Rob

Merry Christmas 2009

Love Mom

Summer Pleasures, Winter Pleasures

Summer Pleasures, Winter Pleasures

A HUDSON VALLEY COOKBOOK

PETER G. ROSE

FRONT COVER: Lunch is served overlooking Haverstraw Bay with a view of Croton Point Park. Chilled lovage soup starts a meal of Hudson Valley cheeses, smoked fish with a horseradish sauce, salad, breads, and a dessert of rice pudding with almond sticks and fruit.

BACK COVER: Coffee and an almond-filled S-shaped puff pastry are waiting by the fire on December 5, Saint Nicholas Eve, an important Dutch celebration.

PHOTOGRAPHS: *Richard Jacobs*; FOOD STYLING: *Peter G. Rose*

Published by
STATE UNIVERSITY OF NEW YORK PRESS, ALBANY

© 2009 Peter G. Rose

Printed in the United States of America

For information, contact
State University of New York Press, Albany, NY
www.sunypress.edu

Production and book design, Laurie Searl
Marketing, Fran Keneston

Library of Congress Cataloging-in-Publication Data

Rose, Peter G.
Summer pleasures, winter pleasures : a Hudson Valley cookbook / Peter G. Rose.
   p. cm.
ISBN 978-1-4384-2987-8 (hardcover : alk. paper)
1. Cookery, American. 2. Cookery—Hudson River Valley (N.Y. and N.J.) I. Title.
TX715.R8337 2009
641.59747'3—dc22
                                                    2009019141

10 9 8 7 6 5 4 3 2 1

to my mother, for the past

to Don, for the present

to Peter Pamela, for the future

Contents

Acknowledgments

For more than twenty years I have written a column on family food for regional papers in the Hudson Valley, particularly the Gannett Newspapers in Westchester, Putnam, and Rockland counties, and contributed articles to regional, national, and international newspapers and magazines. Although in the last five years I have worked on other projects, I have found that readers still remember the recipes and have clipped and saved them. Some of the most popular ones are included in this book.

In the summer, our lives are centered on our patio with a homemade waterfall and our boat *Pot Luck.* Our patio entertaining and boating adventures on the Hudson River and the Erie Canal have resulted in many of the recipes, which I included in the Summer section.

In the winter, our fireplace is the focal point of our lives and friends join us for long evenings by the fire with good conversation and of course good food. From menus for those evenings come the recipes for the Winter section. Throughout the book I have drawn on the Hudson Valley's past and its current active involvement with local farmers and sustainable agriculture. More and more we will all come to realize that New York's Hudson Valley equals California's Napa Valley as an enticing culinary and especially historic destination.

I thank readers and friends who have helped me pick some of the recipes or have given me recipes for the book. My thanks also to Marcia Moss, James Peltz, designer/editor Laurie Searl, and Fran Keneston of Excelsior Editions of SUNY Press, for their help and interest in making this an attractive and appealing book. Richard Jacobs I thank most sincerely for the pleasant collaboration that started more than twenty years ago and for his beautiful photos used in this book and on the cover. Above all, I thank my wonderful husband Don, who makes everything possible.

Summer Pleasures, Winter Pleasures

Part I

SUMMER

PREVIOUS PAGE: A summery buffet with an hors d'oeuvres platter of jicama with chili salt, basil beans, zebras, herring on cucumber slices, deviled eggs, and sea beans (a crunchy green grown in the dunes along the ocean). To the left of the platter, you find a blue cheese ball with almonds (chapter 5—Hors d'oeuvres), as well as grilled meatballs with scallions (chapter 6—Simple main courses), apricot tartlets (chapter 8—Desserts), ginger treats and brown sugar dainties (chapter 9—Cookies), Great-grandma's applesauce cake (chapter 1—Breakfast foods), Rosolje (chapter 3—Salads) and Hudson Valley mustards.

PHOTO: *Richard Jacobs*; FOOD STYLING: *Peter G. Rose*

Introduction

The Hudson Valley's history goes back very far to Native Americans, who for centuries fished in the Hudson River and grew their foods in the valley's fertile grounds. The European history starts with the explorations of Henry Hudson in 1609. He came here, while in the employ of the Dutch East India Company, hoping to find a northerly passage to the Orient. The first Dutch settlers arrived in the first quarter of the seventeenth century and we can still easily find the valley's many Dutch connections—for instance, in its place names, such as Amsterdam, Rotterdam, or even Fishkill (the word *kill*, *kil* in Dutch, means stream). Dutch barns still dot the landscape, as does the typically Dutch architecture of houses such as Van Cortlandt Manor in Croton-on-Hudson. Local museums and historic homes are filled with Dutch artifacts. Some of the recipes in *Summer Pleasures, Winter Pleasures* reflect that Dutch heritage.

As the title indicates, the book celebrates the summer and winter seasons in the Hudson Valley. Whether you sit on your patio and enjoy your yard while the birds are singing and the chipmunks playing or you are out and about on your boat, in a cabin in the woods, or driving your RV along one of the many valley byways, this book is for you. The recipes collected here will help you make mealtime easier; they produce good food without much fuss. Every one of them has been tested repeatedly.

New ideas for breakfast or for take-along sandwiches are always welcome. Soups and salads that use the valley's vegetable bounty are great additions to meats from the grill. What's nicer than to relax at the end of the day with a cool drink and a few nibbles, whether it is herring spread on a cucumber slice or a little more sinful cracker with blue cheese? Simple main courses followed by delicious fruit desserts are the kinds of foods that make summertime so enjoyable.

A pantry shelf stocked with some handy items will make life easier. Here is a short list of foodstuffs that are helpful to have on hand: nuts of any kind; spices, such as ginger, nutmeg, cloves, cinnamon, and especially curry powder; bouillon cubes; pasta, short and long; canned black, white, and kidney beans, as well as canned beets; Hudson Valley mustards or chutneys; canned salmon and pouches of tuna; grains such as couscous, brown rice, or wild rice; dried cranberries, raisins, currants, and apricots.

Day trips to the valley's many special destinations make you feel you have been away for a week and you'll always find some food (or drink) to bring home to make the memories last. The Hudson Valley and Catskill area can boast of at least forty wineries that make wines from grapes and other fruit or produce cider. There are also many microbreweries in the valley, and Tuthilltown Spirits in Gardiner is New York's only whiskey distillery. Plan a visit and combine a winery trip with some local antiquing, a stop at one (of the many) area's historic homes, and finish with a great meal in a local restaurant. Be sure to pick up along the way a complimentary copy of *The Valley Table*, the magazine of Hudson Valley farms, food, and cuisine, to get an update on the latest agricultural and culinary news.

Whether it is a day-trip to Millbrook with its antique shops, winery, and castle; to Kingston with the Senate house, Saturday farmers' market (the best in the valley, in my opinion), and the Rondout waterfront; or a trip to Albany with the New York State Museum and its dioramas of the valley's first inhabitants, various historic homes, and a stop at the city's award-winning microbrewery, the Albany Pump Station—all of these and so many more sightseeing opportunities will leave you with a sense of adventure and a feeling of relaxation and well-being.

Enjoy the season and celebrate with great food!

1

Breakfast foods that make a difference

When we're away on our boat in the Hudson, there is time for a leisurely breakfast, particularly when we're anchored in the recreation area east of Houghtaling Island, opposite New Baltimore, New York. I call the spot my magic kingdom because we can sit in early morning and watch heron and eagles fish for their breakfast while I make ours. Time just floats away in this enchanting place and it is noon before you know it.

Picking our own summer fruit has become a tradition in my small family. Every year we go to Greig Farm in Red Hook or Lawrence Farms Orchards in Newburgh to pick whatever is in season. There are so many wonderful orchards and fruit farms up and down our valley and visiting them makes for a great summer outing.

Baked eggs in toast cups or hollowed-out tomatoes

4 tablespoons butter, melted

6 thin slices bread

A few slices finely cut sandwich ham, optional

6 eggs

Some finely chopped parsley and chives

Preheat oven to 400 degrees. Brush bread slices with melted butter. Press the slices in the cups of a muffin tin. Sprinkle with some of the ham, if used, and break an egg into each cup and top with a little of the herb mixture. Bake for 10–15 minutes, or until the eggs are set. Using the same method, substitute tomatoes for the bread. Hollow out one tomato per person. Turn it upside down to drain. Sprinkle with salt, pepper, and minced fresh herbs (or dried oregano), then break an egg into each tomato. Set each egg-tomato in a custard cup or small ovenproof dish and bake for about 15 minutes or until the egg is set. Sprinkle with more minced herbs, if you have them.

Blueberry/peach coffeecake

1¾ cups all-purpose flour, divided

1 cup sugar, divided

¼ teaspoon freshly grated nutmeg

1 stick (½ cup) butter, melted and cooled, divided

1 teaspoon EACH baking powder and baking soda

¼ teaspoon salt

1 egg, beaten with ½ cup milk

1 teaspoon lemon zest

4 medium peaches, peeled, quartered, and thinly
   sliced across, divided (2 cups)

2 cups blueberries, divided

Preheat oven to 350 degrees. Grease and flour a 9-inch square baking dish.

To prepare crumb mixture: In a small bowl, combine ½ cup flour, ¼ cup sugar, the nutmeg, and 2 tablespoons of melted butter and set aside.

To prepare batter: In a large bowl, mix remaining flour, ½ cup sugar, baking powder and soda, and salt. Add remaining melted butter, milk/egg mixture, and lemon zest. Stir until just blended, then gently stir in half of the fruit and spoon into the prepared pan. Sprinkle with half of the crumb mixture. In a small bowl, mix remaining fruit with ¼ cup sugar and spoon on top and sprinkle remaining crumb mixture over fruit. Bake 50–55 minutes or until golden. Serve warm or at room temperature.

High-bush blueberries are easy to pick and easy to freeze. Usually the four of us get the "most-picked-in-one-day" award with some 40 pounds of fruit, but Jason Harris, our daughter's husband, gets the "neatest picker" prize because, as he picks, he removes all the little stems from the berries. I adapted the coffee cake from a pamphlet by the North American Blueberry Council. The recipe might seem a bit fussy, but it is worth the effort. This moist coffee cake makes a great summer breakfast or a treat anytime.

Fruit scones

2 cups all-purpose flour

¼ cup cornstarch

¼ cup sugar

1 tablespoon baking powder

¼ teaspoon salt

6 tablespoons butter

2 eggs

⅓ cup milk

1 cup chopped nectarines, plums, peeled peaches, whole blueberries, or halved cherries.

Preheat oven to 450 degrees. In a large bowl, sift flour/cornstarch, sugar, baking powder, and salt. With a dough blender or two knives, cut in butter until fine crumbs form, rubbing the crumbs between your fingers to incorporate the butter into the flour mixture. In a small bowl, lightly beat eggs and milk until blended; set aside 1 tablespoon for brushing on finished triangles. Stir remaining egg mixture into flour, mixing with a fork until dough forms, then carefully but with a light touch incorporate the fruit. On a lightly floured surface, knead lightly a few times. With floured hands (dough is sticky) pat dough out into a 6-inch square. Cut into 4 (3 × 3 inch) squares. Cut each of those squares into 2 triangles. Brush with reserved egg mixture and, if you like, sprinkle with some sugar. Place on greased baking sheet and bake for 15 minutes or until golden. Serve warm with butter and preserves (lemon curd is particularly nice). This recipe makes 8 scones.

NOTE:
When you want to make blueberry scones, use frozen berries—that way they will not get squashed in the kneading and color the dough.

Scones are easy to make and yet the result looks like you "fussed." This recipe can be made with whatever summer fruit you have on hand, but you can also use dried fruit, such as cranberries or cherries. Trader Joe's sells a dried "golden berry mix" that makes a nice fruit filling for scones.

Great-grandma's applesauce cake

½ cup butter, softened

½ cup sugar

1 cup applesauce (see below)

1 cup currants

1 cup chopped walnuts

1 cup blueberries (frozen; see note in previous recipe),
optional

2 cups all-purpose flour

1 teaspoon EACH baking soda and cinnamon

½ teaspoon cloves

¼ teaspoon salt

Preheat oven to 350 degrees. Grease a 9-inch square dish or a 6-cup fluted mold.

In an electric mixer, beat butter and sugar until light and fluffy. Add the applesauce. In a small bowl, combine currants, walnuts, and frozen blueberries, if used, with 3 tablespoons of the flour and set aside. Add remaining flour, baking soda, cinnamon, cloves, and salt to butter mixture and combine to make a homogenous batter. Stir in the prepared fruit and nuts and spoon into pan. Bake about 40 minutes or until a knife inserted comes out clean.

Over the years I have tried many applesauce cakes, but this old-fashioned version gets my vote for number one. It is best made with your own applesauce, which is easy to do as follows: peel, core, and quarter 3 apples such as Golden Delicious, Jonagold, or Ida Red (each imparts its own distinctive flavor). Cook with ⅓ cup water until soft and mash.

Sunshine eggs

5 slices, at least ½ inch thick, of multigrain or Italian bread

½ cup shredded sharp cheddar cheese

Cooked and crumbled breakfast sausage

(or use chopped ham), optional

5 eggs

1 cup milk

1 tablespoon coarse grain mustard

¼ cup minced chives or scallions with greens

Handful of chopped parsley and leaves of 2 sprigs fresh

marjoram, if available (or ½ teaspoon dried marjoram)

¼ teaspoon EACH salt and freshly ground pepper

Grease a 1-quart baking dish. Cut bread into cubes. Toss with the cheese and meat, if used, in the baking dish. Use a whisk to thoroughly beat together the eggs, milk, mustard, salt, pepper, and all the herbs and pour over bread mixture.

Cover and refrigerate for several hours or overnight. To bake: preheat oven to 350 degrees. Bake covered for 45–50 minutes or until golden brown.

When you have company staying overnight, knowing that breakfast is taken care of before you go to bed makes you sleep better, I think. This recipe is a great way of using up stale bread and a nice change from French toast. Add some summer fruit and a good cup of coffee or tea and leisurely enjoy yourself.

2

Sandwiches to enjoy at home or to take along

A ziplock bag tightly packed with ice cubes or a frozen cold pack are handy ways to keep things cold when you are going on a picnic. Here are five recipes for sandwich fillings that are a nice change from the usual cold cuts. The first recipe comes from the archives of Wilderstein, a beautiful Queen Anne style house along the Hudson in Rhinebeck. Robert Suckley, its owner, was also its "secret cook." While he cooked the meals for family and guests, he never let on that he had done so. There are scrapbooks of his recipes and many of his printed cookbooks in Wilderstein's archives. The recipe for chicken salad that follows was among them.

Chicken salad with sliced almonds

1 cup chopped cooked chicken

3 tablespoons mayonnaise

2 tablespoons cream or milk

¼ teaspoon EACH salt, paprika, and freshly ground pepper

½ cup chopped blanched almonds or sliced almonds

Butter at room temperature

6 slices bread of your choice

In a small bowl, combine the first 5 ingredients. Carefully butter the bread and spread on the filling. Cut in half for sandwiches. If used as tea sandwiches, remove the crust and cut into quarters. This recipe makes 3 sandwiches.

Chime sandwich, open-faced

Whole wheat or multigrain bread slices

Butter

Sharp cheddar cheese slices

Ripe tomatoes, sliced

Salt and pepper

Basil leaves, rinsed and chopped

Butter the bread. Top with cheese, then tomato slices, and season with salt and pepper. Sprinkle thickly with chopped basil. This is summer in a bite!

The first boat we had on the Hudson River was called Wind Chime. We did not have it very long because it proved to be too small, since neither one of us could stand up in it and the galley area was simply too tiny to be able to cook a real meal. On our first trip from Croton-on-Hudson to Albany (and back) we brought some of our garden's bounty along and that's how these sandwiches were "invented."

Ham, egg, and asparagus sandwich spread

10 asparagus, washed and hard ends broken off; cut into 3 or 4 pieces

6 slices sandwich ham

2 hard-boiled eggs, peeled and cut in half

¼ teaspoon EACH salt and pepper

⅓ cup mayonnaise

1 teaspoon lemon juice

1 scallion, minced

Bring a saucepan with water to a boil. Drop in the asparagus and allow to cook for 2 minutes and remove. Place all ingredients in food processor outfitted with a metal blade and process to make a chunky spread. Spread on whole grain or white bread. I do not think buttering the bread is necessary.

By June there will be asparagus available, grown in the Hudson Valley. Some farms allow you to pick them; others sell them at their farm stands. Use them in the delicate sandwich spread above that is made in no time in a food processor.

Herb spread with salami

8 ounces reduced-fat cream cheese, or use thick Greek
yogurt

8 radishes, finely chopped

3 carrots, scraped, cut into thin sticks and then finely
chopped

5 scallions, finely chopped with most of their greens

¼ cup minced parsley

¼ cup minced fresh mint

Salt and freshly ground pepper to taste

Milk or cream for thinning, as necessary

Combine all ingredients; if the mixture is too thick, add some milk or cream to make it of spreading consistency. Spread on whole grain bread and top with salami slices. For a vegetarian sandwich: top with sliced tomatoes and avocado, lightly drizzled with lemon juice to help retain its color.

A delicious herb spread made with garden herbs can be used in many different ways: as the base of a sandwich (as you can see in the recipe above), as a spread with crackers, or even as a filling for cherry tomatoes or celery sticks.

Vidalia onion, tomatoes, and olives spread

1 tablespoon olive oil

1 large Vidalia onion, sliced in half-circles

3 cloves garlic, minced (or less)

5 plum tomatoes, sliced lengthwise in half and then into half-circles

½ cup or more parsley, chopped

¼ cup dry white wine, or use water

½ cup sliced black olives

Just a little sugar; salt and freshly ground pepper

Romaine or lettuce leaves and whole wheat pitas

Heat oil and fry onions until lightly browned and limp. Stir in garlic, tomatoes, parsley, and wine or water and allow mixture to cook down on simmer for about 15 minutes. Do not cover the pan. Stir occasionally. When almost all the liquid has evaporated and the vegetables are soft and tender, stir in the olives and allow to heat through for a few more minutes. Sprinkle on a little bit of sugar to reduce the tomatoes' acidity and season with salt and freshly ground pepper to taste. To assemble: line a pita with a large Romaine lettuce leaf folded in half and fill with the mixture. Serve either warm or at room temperature.

3

Salads, with fresh or cooked vegetables

In summer the valley's farmers' markets are overflowing with large assortments of greens and crisp cucumbers. When you're used to waxed supermarket cucumbers and bite into a freshly picked one, the taste and texture are a revelation. Those cucumbers are crisp, slightly sweet, and juicy. Now is the time to enjoy this seasonal bonus.

The first salad recipe uses summer's abundance of basil to best advantage. Put the beans in a jar as indicated and bring it along to a pot luck or picnic. At Montgomery Place in Annandale-on-Hudson, picnics "are encouraged." Its beautiful grounds with scenic views of the river are the perfect locale for outdoor eating, and afterwards you can follow a trail to a roaring waterfall or go to a nearby farm stand for goodies to bring home. Another quite enchanting place for a stroll or a picnic (in designated areas only) is Innisfree Garden in Millbrook. In this 150-acre public garden, according to its website, "the ancient art of Chinese landscape design has been reinterpreted to create a unique American garden."

You will love your visit.

Basil beans

1 cup cider or white wine vinegar

4–5 tablespoons sugar

¼ teaspoon EACH salt and freshly ground pepper

½ pound haricots verts (thin green beans) or regular green beans, tipped and toed

15–20 basil leaves, cut into thin strips just before cooking

2 tablespoons minced parsley

In a medium saucepan, bring the cider (or vinegar), sugar, salt, and pepper to a boil. Add the beans and cook 2–3 minutes for thin beans; 3–4 minutes for regular beans. Remove from heat; add basil and combine thoroughly. Cool slightly and put into a regular screwtop jar. Add the parsley, cover, and shake. Open the jar and allow to cool completely before closing. Store in refrigerator and use as a summery hors d'oeuvre, side dish, or to take along on a picnic.

Cucumber and radish salad

2 cucumbers, peeled and cut in half lengthwise

6 large radishes

3 scallions, finely chopped with most of their tops

Dressing

⅓ cup white wine or white distilled vinegar

¼ cup vegetable oil

½ teaspoon sugar

1 teaspoon salt

¼ teaspoon freshly ground pepper

With a spoon, remove seeds from cucumber halves and cut cucumbers into ½-inch slices. Cut off ends and tops of the radishes and slice them into small sticks. In a medium bowl, combine cucumbers, radishes, and scallions. In a jar or bowl, combine dressing ingredients and pour onto the vegetables. Stir and allow to stand for 1 hour before serving.

The combination of red radishes and light green cucumber is not only pretty but also tasty. The peppery radishes accent the cukes. When the salad stands, it turns an appealing pink.

Carley's zucchini salad

Salad

5–8 medium zucchini, sliced about ¼ inch thick

4 scallions, sliced thin, including most of the green tops

½ cup celery, finely chopped

½ cup red or green peppers, or some of both, finely chopped

Dressing

⅔ cup white distilled, white wine, or rice wine vinegar

¾ cup sugar

½ cup vegetable oil

1 teaspoon salt

In a large bowl, combine the vegetables. In a small bowl, combine the dressing ingredients and pour onto the salad mixture. Marinate the salad at least 3 hours or overnight. Carley notes that the salad keeps crisp for 2 weeks. (I store my leftovers in empty pickle jars in the refrigerator.)

NOTE: Use zucchini not only in bread or as a vegetable, but in salad, soup, as part of a vegetable Reuben sandwich, or in ratatouille.

When we are in Kingston on our boat Pot Luck, lots of friends come for a visit. Kingston's Rondout is a very pleasant place to dock and watch the waterfront activity. A favorite guest is Esell Hoenshell-Watson, who owns the Alternative Baker, now in Rosendale, New York. We just love his bread, sandwiches, and his large butterscotch cookies, among the many other delicious items he prepares. One night he brought his mom, Carley Watson, to the boat and we talked for hours about food and cooking. Clearly, Esell got his culinary skills from his mother; she gave me the recipe above. I was delighted to find another way to use summer's unlimited bounty of zucchini.

Grandma's four bean salad

Salad

2 cups briefly cooked green beans (see note)

2 cups briefly cooked yellow beans (see note)

1 can (15.5 ounces) kidney beans, drained

1 can (15.5 ounces) chickpeas, drained or use cranberry beans (see below)

1 cup celery, scraped to remove threads and finely diced

½ cup finely chopped scallions

Dressing

⅔ cup white wine or white distilled vinegar

⅓ cup vegetable oil

¾ cup sugar

1 teaspoon salt

½ teaspoon freshly ground pepper

1 teaspoon celery seed, crushed with a rolling pin to release flavor

In a small bowl, combine dressing ingredients. In a large bowl, combine all beans, celery, and scallions. Stir in dressing and allow to stand for at least 1 hour, so flavors can marry.

NOTE:

Bring a pot of water to a boil and drop in both green and yellow beans. Return to boil and cook for 3 minutes. Remove beans with a slotted spoon and cool for use in the salad.

This is the way my mother-in-law made her bean salad; of course for camping or boating this dish can be made entirely from canned vegetables. I prefer as many fresh ones as possible and over the years I have discovered the fall crop of cranberry beans at Hudson Valley farm stands. I do not mind the shelling of these mottled red and beige beans or cooking them; they only take 15–20 minutes and are so worth the effort.

Rosolje (Estonian herring salad)

1 jar pickled herring (small or large, depending on how much you like herring)

4 medium cooked potatoes (2 cups cubed)

6 large beets, cooked and peeled (about 4½ cups when cubed)

½ pound baked ham, roast pork, or cooked veal (about 2 cups cubed)

2 large tart Granny Smith apples (2 cups cubed)

1 small onion, peeled and minced

3 large sour pickles (2 cups cubed)

6 peeled hard-boiled eggs, 4 diced and 2 whole

Cube the herring. In a large bowl, combine all ingredients, but set aside ½ cup cubed beets and the 2 whole eggs for the topping. Then prepare the dressing, as follows.

The Hudson Valley has an enormously varied population. I am fortunate to have an Estonian neighbor, Elve Muursepp, who is willing to share her country's recipes. Elve gave me the recipe for this herring salad (it will be the best one you have ever had, I guarantee). In keeping with tradition, serve it with a nice crusty loaf of bread. She explained to me that her cuisine reflects the history of this Baltic country. Each invader left a mark, and the food combines elements from other countries. The most important food is bread, which is revered. The customs that spring from that reverence include kissing a piece of bread that has fallen on the floor.

Dressing

1½ cups sour cream

½ cup mayonnaise

3 teaspoons prepared mustard

1 teaspoon sugar, or more if you like a sweet-and-sour taste

1 tablespoon lemon juice

4 tablespoons fresh dill, chopped

Salt and freshly ground pepper, to taste

In a small bowl, combine dressing ingredients and taste for seasoning. Correct if necessary. Combine with salad ingredients. The salad should be moist, not wet. Chill the salad in a serving bowl for at least 4 hours or overnight. When ready to serve, finely chop the reserved ½ cup of cubed beets. Chop the yolks and whites of the reserved eggs separately. Arrange in triangular patterns on top of the salad (see photo of Summer dishes, page 1). This recipe serves at least 8–10, but can easily be cut in half.

4

Soups, cold for a hot summer's day

L ike cold drinks, cold soups can be reviving (and nourishing) on a summer's day. Here are five different versions from a–z (asparagus to zucchini) with broccoli and tarragon, cucumber and avacoado, and melon and strawberry in between. They make a delicious snack or pick-me-up, but can also be served as an interesting first course for lunch or dinner. The first recipe, for example, makes a simple, yet elegant starter to a seafood dinner of grilled shrimp or lobster.

Chilled asparagus soup

3 cups water

1 teaspoon EACH salt and sugar

1 bunch green asparagus, washed, hard ends removed,
    broken into 3 or 4 pieces

¼ cup minced fresh parsley

¼ teaspoon freshly grated nutmeg

2 cups half-and-half or milk

4 tablespoons finely chopped smoked salmon for garnish,
    optional

In a medium saucepan, bring the water to a boil, season with salt and sugar, and drop in the asparagus. Cook for 3 minutes, add parsley, and cook 1 minute more. Use an immersion blender or regular blender to puree the mixture. Season with nutmeg and cool. Stir in milk or half-and-half. Divide between 4 bowls and garnish each with a tablespoon of the salmon.

Chilled broccoli and tarragon soup

2 tablespoons vegetable oil

2 shallots, peeled and minced (if you wish, you could substitute 3 scallions)

3 tablespoons chopped fresh tarragon

2 cups cooked broccoli

3 cups cooking water

3 boiled medium potatoes

1 cup heavy cream or half-and-half

Salt and freshly ground pepper

In a small frying pan, heat oil and fry shallots until translucent. Add the chopped tarragon and cook just until wilted. Remove from heat. In a blender, combine the shallot mixture, broccoli, cooking water, and potatoes. Process until fairly smooth. The soup can be made a day or so ahead. Refrigerate to chill. To serve, stir in the cream and add salt and pepper.

Tarragon, with its licorice taste, is the perfect accent for broccoli as you will see in this recipe.

Chilled cucumber and avocado soup

1 long European cucumber or 2 regular cucumbers, peeled

1 ripe avocado

3 tablespoons chopped parsley

3 scallions, chopped with most of their greens

¼ teaspoon red pepper flakes

Salt and freshly ground pepper

2 tablespoons lemon juice

¼ cup water

Cut cucumber(s) in half lengthwise, clean out seeds with a spoon, and cut into chunks. Cut avocado in half, remove pit, and scrape out flesh with a spoon. Combine all ingredients in a blender and blend until fairly smooth. Taste and adjust seasonings. Put blender container in the refrigerator until ready to serve.

I am assuming that you have a blender to make a pina colada, margarita, daiquiri, or other drinks for a hot summer's day. Now is the time to use it for this very refreshing soup that makes a delicious start for a patio meal of grilled meats and salad.

Chilled curried zucchini soup

4 cups zucchini (see below)

1 tablespoon vegetable oil

2 tablespoons minced onion

¼ teaspoon dried marjoram

2 tablespoons flour

4 cups beef broth

¼–½ teaspoon curry powder

Salt and freshly ground pepper

2 tablespoons chopped parsley

Heavy cream or half-and-half, optional

Cut each zucchini into 8 (or more if necessary) thin strips and then into tiny slivers by cutting across. Heat the oil and add zucchini, onion, and marjoram. Cook, while stirring, for 3 minutes. Sprinkle the flour onto this mixture and combine completely. Slowly add beef broth and, when all is added, cook for 3 more minutes. Taste and season with pepper and salt. Add ¼ teaspoon of curry powder, stir, and taste again, adding more if necessary. (Some curry powders are very strongly flavored and you do not want to overpower the zucchini taste.) Stir in the parsley and cook a few minutes longer. Use an immersion blender or regular blender and process the soup until fairly smooth. Remove and cool. Serve with a dash of cream in each bowl, if desired.

This summer soup is a family favorite I have made for at least thirty years. It freezes well and, as an added benefit, uses some of that persistent zucchini crop.

Chilled melon/strawberry soup with champagne

1 cantaloupe melon, cut in half, seeds removed

1 pint strawberries, washed, hulls removed, and sliced

    (set aside 6 berries for garnish)

Juice of 1 orange

Juice of ½ lemon

Chilled champagne

Peel melon and cut into chunks. In a blender, combine melon with strawberries and the orange and lemon juices and puree. Serve in glass bowls or crystal glasses. Top each serving with a few strawberry slices. Pass the champagne bottle so that everyone can add a dash to their soup and serve the rest in sparkling champagne flutes.

Save the recipe above for one of those warm flower-scented evenings in June when the strawberries are ripe at local farms. The next course of what promises to be a romantic meal could be smoked salmon with a horseradish sauce (mayonnaise or sour cream mixed with store-bought, beet-flavored horseradish to taste) and a salad of lovely greens, cucumbers, and tomatoes, along with good, crusty bread. To give this meal an indulgent ending, serve chocolate gelato or ice cream with butter cookies and bonbons for dessert.

5

Hors d'oeuvres or anytime snacks

The following five recipes will make an enticing tray of finger foods for a small patio party. I confess that the first one has been a standby for a long time, but all my friends love it and so, I believe, will you. For a cheese board, pair it with a valley "treasure," Hudson Valley Camembert, made by the Old Chatham Sheepherding Company in Chatham and garnish with fruits from the local farmers' market. Or try any of the other the cow's milk, or goat or sheep's milk cheeses lovingly made in the Hudson Valley.

Blue cheese ball with almonds

About ⅓ cup whole almonds

4 ounces blue cheese (Danish blue, Stilton, or Gorgonzola)
at room temperature

8 ounces (reduced-fat) cream cheese at room temperature

Preheat oven to 300 degrees. Place almonds on a baking sheet and toast for 10 minutes. Remove and cool. In a bowl, combine blue cheese and cream cheese, using a fork to mash them together (or use an electric mixer). If necessary, add a tablespoon or so of milk. Use plastic wrap to help you form the mixture into a ball and cover the entire outside with whole almonds. It looks nice and tastes wonderful.

Deviled eggs with Hudson Valley mustard

2 hard-boiled eggs, cut in half lengthwise and yolks removed

1 teaspoon mustard, ZAZ or any other brand (see below)

1 teaspoon mayonnaise

Salt and freshly ground pepper

Caviar (an inexpensive brand is fine for this use)

This recipe can be multiplied, of course.

Mash the yolks and combine with mustard and mayonnaise and salt and pepper. Fill the cavities of the whites with the mixture and top with a spoonful of caviar.

Mustard enhances salad dressings, soups, and entrees. It tastes good on a sandwich, a pretzel, a burger, or a frank at a ball game and serves as a dip for cubes of cheese. It stimulates salivary secretion and aids in digestion. In the New Testament, mustard seeds are a symbol of faith and in other cultures the seeds are thought of as symbols of fertility.

Hudson Valley mustard makers have come up with their own versions. Grey Mouse Farms in Saugerties makes a horseradish mustard that is a hot, flavorful mixture, perfect for a ham or roast beef sandwich. John King of Hudson Valley Homestead produces a delicious maple-walnut mustard among others, and ZAZ mustards in Big Indian come "with a kick" or a "kick and a half." Those mustards are mixed with brown sugar to make a sweet, lush condiment. I like to use ZAZ in deviled eggs and top them with some caviar. It is a wonderful combination of sweet, creamy, and salty tastes.

Jicama with chili salt

Jicama, peeled and cut into sticks

2 teaspoons chili powder

1 teaspoon salt

Serve the jicama sticks with a small dish of the chili powder mixed with the salt. Dip and eat!

NOTE:
My friend Andrea Candee purees dates, mint, and lime juice in a blender and serves the resulting paste on jicama slices—a truly refreshing treat.

Nowadays, with everyone dieting, you cannot serve a snack tray without including a fruit or a vegetable. It is a fine way to use the abundance of the valley's fruit and vegetables, but I am also very fond of crunchy jicama and serve it as described above. Another lesser known vegetable to add to the tray is the sea-bean, which looks like green coral but actually grows in the dunes along the ocean (see photo of Summer dishes on page 1—on the red platter, the sea beans are on the right.) Long white radishes and melon sticks also make interesting additions.

Kippered herring spread
on cucumber slices

1 cucumber, peeled and cut into ½-inch slices

1 (3–3.5 ounce) can kippered boneless herring fillets, drained

1 hard-boiled egg, peeled and cut in half lengthwise

2 scallions, finely chopped

2 tablespoons minced parsley

3 tablespoons mayonnaise or a little more as necessary

¼ teaspoon freshly ground pepper

In a shallow bowl, mash the herring and egg halves with a fork. Add the scallions, parsley, mayonnaise, pepper, and combine. Spoon onto cucumber slices and serve.

This is another one of my summer standbys that is well liked. It is particularly handy on a boat or for happy hour at the end of a long day in the RV.

Zebras (whole grain bread with butter and Gouda cheese)

Dark rye bread squares or similar bread (see below)

Butter

Gouda cheese (cut thickly, as indicated below)

Butter the bread slices. Cut the cheese in slices as thick as the bread; this is important for achieving the striped zebra effect. Top the bread with a cheese slice and cover with another buttered bread slice. Cut into 2 x 1-inch fingers and serve. Simple, yet delicious.

Traditionally, zebras are triple-decker sandwich squares, but I have found that they stay together better on an hors d'oeuvres tray in regular sandwich form. The bread you use for these is a square German rye or a Dutch roggebrood. Spelt or "health" bread in that shape is also good. Supermarkets usually have those kinds of square, dense breads in their deli section.

6

Simple main courses

With three recipes for the grill and two prepared in the oven, there are enough ideas in this chapter for any kind of summer day. You can make the meatballs in the next recipe as spicy as you like by adding some red pepper flakes. Wild rice or couscous (see next chapter) make tasty accompaniments. For a patio party, the recipe can be doubled, or you could serve both the meatballs and the turkey skewers for variety.

Grilled meatballs with scallions, Turkish style

1 pound ground beef

1 slice hearty whole wheat bread,
  soaked in a little water and squeezed dry

1 small egg or half of a beaten large egg

½ teaspoon curry powder

¼ teaspoon ground ginger

Salt and pepper, to taste

18 scallions or more, washed

IMPORTANT:
Use a spatula when carefully turning skewers to ensure that they hold together.

Cut off all of the white part of the scallions and about ½ inch of the greens, these will be used to skewer alternately with the meatballs. Finely chop the leftover greens from the scallions and mix 3 tablespoons with the meat.

Use wooden skewers and soak them in water for half an hour before using. In a medium bowl, thoroughly combine beef, bread, egg, finely chopped scallion greens, and seasonings. Shape into 2-inch oblong meatballs. On skewers, alternate meatballs (lengthwise) with scallion pieces (crosswise). Start and end with scallions. Brush the scallions with a little vegetable oil. Spray or brush the grill with oil. Grill the skewers as you would grill burgers: about 8–10 minutes on a medium hot grill.

Grilled striped bass fillets

2 tablespoons olive oil

1 clove garlic, minced

1 large tomato, finely chopped

1 tablespoon capers

6–8 basil leaves, torn

Dash white wine

Salt and freshly ground pepper

2 thick fillets of bass, rinsed and dried

In a frying pan, heat olive oil and add garlic, tomato, and capers. Cook over medium heat for 5 minutes; add basil and white wine and cook together 5 minutes more. Season lightly with salt and freshly ground pepper. Place the bass fillet on a medium grill, skin side down, and heap the tomato mixture on top. Cover the grill and cook for 20 minutes. Leftover sauce may be poured on at serving time.

Whenever I have a question about fish, I turn to seafood sage Joe DiMauro of Mount Kisco Seafood. He gave me the recipe above for grilling the quintessential Hudson River fish, striped bass. Often when our boat is anchored in the river we are awoken in early morning by the roar of bass boats blasting by. Some years ago when we were docked at Riverview Marina in Catskill, New York, we attended the prize ceremony of the National Bass Fishing Contest and watched as the various catches were weighed. It was a fun occasion, held at Catskill Point, a beautiful tiny park that juts out into the river. During the summer it is also the spot where the Catskill farmers' market is held, which not only has a large assortment of products, but also a band that plays cheerful Dixieland music to everyone's delight.

Grilled turkey and nectarine kebabs

1 pound boneless turkey, cut into 1-inch cubes

4 firm nectarines, cut into large wedges

⅓ cup soy sauce

2 tablespoons olive oil

3 tablespoons honey

1 scant tablespoon finely minced fresh ginger

Alternate turkey and nectarine wedges on metal skewers. Brush with the sauce made by combining soy sauce, oil, honey, and ginger. Place skewers on a rack 4 inches above medium-hot coals. Grill about 5 minutes; turn and grill 5 minutes longer or just until turkey is cooked. Brush frequently with sauce while grilling.

Nectarines are not only grown in California, they are also grown in the Hudson Valley. In summer they replace apples and quince as my favorite fruits for cooking because they retain their shape and their flavors intensify when cooked.

Mushroom quiche without a crust

10 ounces white mushrooms, wiped clean

1 clove garlic, minced

¼ teaspoon EACH freshly ground pepper, salt, and dried

   marjoram

2 tablespoons minced parsely

1 cup grated Gouda cheese, such as Old Amsterdam

3 eggs, lightly beaten with a ⅓ cup of milk

Preheat oven to 375 degrees. Break off mushroom stems and chop. In a large bowl, combine stems, garlic, seasoning (taste the cheese, if it does not seem salty, add a little more salt to the mixture), cheese, and eggs. Place mushroom caps, opening up, in a 9-inch pie plate in an even layer and pour the egg mixture over the caps. Bake for 10 minutes at 375 degrees and reduce heat to 325 degrees and bake for 30 minutes or until set. Cut into wedges and serve.

The recipe above for a crustless mushroom pie goes back to the seventeenth century. My adaptation makes a perfect dish for a light summer lunch. Serve it with a mixed salad of leafy greens, cucumber, tomatoes, lots of fresh herbs, and perhaps a (rinsed) nasturtium flower or two as garnish. When using edible flowers such as nasturtiums or violets, make sure they have not been sprayed with fertilizer or other chemicals.

Salmon patties from the Sharing Community

1 tablespoon parsley flakes or 2 tablespoons minced fresh parsley

1 teaspoon onion powder or 1 tablespoon minced onion

Pinch red pepper flakes

½ cup mayonnaise

1 egg

Juice of half a lemon

1 15½-ounce can salmon

About 10–12 crushed crackers (Triscuit whole grain wheat crackers work well)

1 cup toasted bread crumbs or Panko

Preheat oven to 400 degrees. In a medium bowl, mix parsley, onion, pepper flakes, mayonnaise, egg, and lemon juice. Stir in the salmon and add enough crackers to make firm patties. Roll in fine bread crumbs. Generously grease a baking sheet; place patties on the sheet and bake for 30 minutes.

Years ago I watched the chefs at the Sharing Community, Inc., in Yonkers, New York, cook for hundreds of hungry people, who line up early to get a place at the table. These cooks need to be inventive to use the foodstuffs available to them wisely and well. This recipe is one of theirs. Add coleslaw and some good bread for a simple summer meal that I guarantee you'll enjoy. It is an ideal meal for a boat or RV.

7

Vegetables and grains

With an alphabet of vegetables at our fingertips from asparagus, beans, beets, broccoli, carrots, celery, corn, cucumbers, eggplant, fennel, greens, leeks, peas, peppers, radishes, swiss chard, tomatoes, and zucchini, we will never lack for variety in this season. Grains and starches can vary as much as vegetables in a summery menu. Couscous is a handy grain because it is so quickly made and should be a pantry staple for RVs or boats. Adding dried cranberries and chopped walnuts (other good standbys) gives extra flavor and crunch.

Couscous with dried cranberries and walnuts

1 cup chicken broth (made from a bouillon cube,
   if necessary)

1 cup couscous

2 scallions, very finely chopped

2 tablespoons dried cranberries

2 or 3 tablespoons chopped walnuts

Heat chicken broth to boiling and stir in couscous, scallions, and cranberries. Remove from heat, cover, and allow to stand for 10 minutes or until all liquid is absorbed. Stir in walnuts and serve.

Grilled corn

6 ears of corn

6 tablespoons of butter, softened

Pull back the husk of each ear, but keep the leaves attached at the bottom. Carefully remove all silk and spread each ear with a tablespoon of butter. Pull up husk and tie with kitchen string about 2 to 3 inches from the top. Soak prepared ears in a large pot of cold water, or in the sink, for at least half an hour. Grill, turning occasionally with tongs, for about 15 minutes or until lightly charred. Cut strings, pull off the husks, and serve.

August is the month for corn. Try grilling it—although the preparation is messy, it can all be done outside and saves you from heating your kitchen with that large pot of boiling water.

Little red potatoes
with butter, parsley, and chives

2–3 tablespoons olive or vegetable oil

1½ pounds small red potatoes, boiled

3 tablespoons each parsley and chives

Salt and freshly ground pepper

In a frying pan, heat the oil. Add potatoes and brown them while stirring. Sprinkle with parsley and chives and season with salt and pepper. Stir to combine and cook a few minutes more to wilt the herbs. An alternative method is to skewer the potatoes on metal skewers, brush them with oil, and grill until browned. Make sure to turn the skewers frequently and brush with oil as necessary. When done, sprinkle with herbs, season them, and serve hot.

Any early potato can be used for the recipe above, but the little red ones are the prettiest. This simple dish makes such a nice change in summer meals when you have been eating a lot of salads. It goes well with grilled meats.

Ratatouille with anise seed

2 tablespoons vegetable oil

2 cloves garlic, peeled and minced

1 large onion, peeled and chopped

1 small eggplant (about 1 pound) cut into ½-inch cubes

1 EACH red, yellow, and green pepper, seeded and sliced

2 zucchini, sliced (about 2 cups)

4 tomatoes, diced

1 tablespoon anise seeds (more if you like), crushed with a

    rolling pin

2 bay leaves

⅓ cup fresh basil leaves, sliced

Salt and freshly ground pepper to taste

In a large deep frying pan or a large saucepan, heat the oil and gently cook garlic and onion until onion is translucent. Add eggplant, peppers, zucchini, tomatoes, anise seeds, bay leaves, and basil. Cover the pan and simmer gently for about 20–30 minutes. Taste and add salt and pepper. Do not overcook or the dish will be mushy.

If you are like me and love mint, licorice, and anise—all related tastes—you'll like the addition of anise seeds to the above vegetable mixture. Together with the minty basil, they give it a bright and lively flavor.

Wild rice with bacon and toasted pecans

1 cup wild rice

2½ cups water, salted to taste

4 slices thick slab bacon

1 teaspoon orange zest

⅓ cup pecans

WARNING:
Do not add more zest than indicated without tasting!

In a saucepan, bring water to a boil and add rice. Cook over low heat for about 50 minutes or until the kernels puff open and the rice has more or less cooked dry; cover and allow to stand so that it will absorb the rest of the water. In the meantime, heat oven to 300 degrees and toast the pecans on a baking sheet for about 10 minutes. Cool and chop. In a frying pan or in the microwave, cook bacon until crispy. Pat bacon slices with paper towels to remove grease and crumble. Just before serving, mix bacon, orange zest, and pecans with the rice and serve.

The nutty taste of wild rice in this recipe is enhanced by the bacon, while the orange zest brightens the combination.

8

Desserts—(not so) sinful, sweet indulgences

Fruits are the jewels of summer, so let's use them as much as possible. They are readily available at the farmers' markets or the orchards of the Hudson Valley. Picking your own berries, peaches, or apples can be combined with sightseeing to make a day's outing. Greig Farm in Red Hook has long been a favorite of ours and lunch at the stately Beekman Arms in the heart of Rhinebeck is the bonus of the trip.

Apricot tartlets

Tartlets

2 cups flour

⅓ cup light brown sugar, firmly packed

11 tablespoons salted butter

2 egg yolks, lightly beaten with a fork

Combine flour, sugar, and butter in a food processor and process until crumbs form. Add the yolks and continue processing until dough hangs together. Remove and neatly press small chunks of dough into small tartlet shells, smooth the rims, and set aside. Preheat oven to 350 degrees.

Apricot filling

Apricots

Sugar

½ pint heavy cream whipped with 3–4 tablespoons of sugar

Use 3 or 4 apricot halves per shell, depending on the shell size. Place apricots in a saucepan and add sugar to taste and enough water to cover the bottom of the pan. Bring to a boil and cook gently just long enough to soften the fruit. Cool. In the meantime, place the tartlets on a baking sheet and bake for about 20–25 minutes or until light brown. Remove and cool. Take the tartlets from their shells and fill with apricot halves and just a little of the juices. Serve with some whipped cream. These tartlets can also be made successfully with commercially canned apricots.

NOTE:

To freeze apricots, wash fruit, cut in half, and remove pit. Let dry and place in freezer bags.

I was very excited to discover that at Laurence Farm Orchards in Newburgh you can pick your own apricots. Every year, we pick at least thirty pounds. We eat some, cook some, and freeze many for a winter's day when those tangy fruits will taste so good. Apricots combine very well with the buttery short crust pastry above. It is quickly made in a food processor and you can watch television while you press the dough into small tartlet shells.

Frozen nectarine pie

3 firm nectarines, washed and cut into large wedges

⅓ cup Creme de Cassis (see note)

½ cup sugar

½ pint heavy whipping cream

8 ounces plain yogurt

1 9-inch commercial chocolate crumb crust

Process the nectarine chunks in a food processor until very finely minced. Or mince finely with a knife. Combine minced nectarines with the liqueur and sugar and let stand for about 15 minutes. In the meantime, stiffly whip the cream, add the yogurt, and combine. Drain the fruit (set the liquid aside), add drained fruit to the cream/yogurt mixture, and combine. Add some of the liquid—the mixture should remain fairly thick. (Any leftover liquid can be combined later with white wine for an extra flavorful Kir to benefit the cook!) Pour the fruit/cream mixture into the crumb shell. For summer convenience, use a commercial baked (chocolate) crumb shell and open the aluminum edge all around so that it will safely hold the filling. Cover with a double layer of plastic wrap and carefully transfer to the freezer and freeze overnight. Remove 10 minutes before serving and lift the pie from the aluminum shell onto a pretty platter. Cut into wedges and serve.

NOTE:
You can use any red fruit liqueur such as Chambord or Strawberry Liqueur.

You can also substitute peaches or berries in this recipe. It is fun to experiment with summer's fruit.

Mother's cake

½ cup (1 stick) butter, softened

1 cup sugar

3 egg yolks, lightly beaten with a fork

1 cup milk

3 cups flour sifted together with 2 teaspoons baking powder

2 teaspoons grated lemon zest

Juice of half lemon

3 egg whites, beaten stiff

1 cup currants, washed, patted dry with paper towels,
and mixed with 1 tablespoon flour

Preheat oven to 325 degrees. Cream butter and sugar, then add the egg yolks and milk. Combine thoroughly, then add the flour and baking powder mixture a little at a time. Stir in the lemon zest and juice and fold in the egg white until just incorporated. Finally, stir in currants. Butter a 9-inch tube pan and carefully spoon in the dough. Bake for about 1 hour and 15 minutes until done and top springs back when touched lightly with a finger. Serve surrounded by garden violets or pansies (make sure they have not been treated with chemicals) or simply dusted with confectioners' sugar. This cake makes a particularly nice accompaniment to a frosty glass of Roman punch (see chapter 10 for that recipe).

The Hudson River Museum in Yonkers is another of the many gems in the valley. It consists of a modern building, a planetarium, and the Glenview Mansion, which it has occupied since 1924 when it was known as the Yonkers Museum of Science and Arts. The mansion was built by John Bond Trevor for his second wife Emily Norwood and their young children. Trevor's grandson still owns a handwritten cookbook with recipes that were served in the mansion. I adapted this recipe from that book. Flavored with lemon and currants, the cake is not as solid as a pound cake yet has a velvety crumb.

Prune plum parfait

1 pound prune plums, cut in half and pits removed

2–3 tablespoons sugar

¼ cup water

½ teaspoon ground cinnamon

Vanilla ice cream

4 crisp cookies, homemade or store-bought

2 tablespoons chopped almonds

In a medium saucepan, combine plums, sugar, water, and cinnamon and bring to a boil. Reduce heat and cover, cooking for 5 minutes or until plums have softened and given off their juices. Remove and cool. When ready to serve, layer plums alternately with small scoops of vanilla ice cream in tall glasses, ending with plums. Crumble the cookies, mix with almonds, and sprinkle on top. Serve with a long spoon.

August is not only the month for corn, but it is also the time when prune plums— sometimes called Italian plums—are ripe. They are another fruit that benefits from cooking. Use them in the this parfait for a fun dessert, loved by young and old.

Rhubarb with raspberries

1 pound rhubarb, stringy parts removed and cut into 1-inch
    pieces

½ cup sugar or less

Half of 12-ounce bag of frozen raspberries

In a medium saucepan, combine rhubarb and sugar with enough water to cover the bottom of the pan. Bring to a boil over high heat. Stir and cook for just a few minutes—rhubarb cooks quickly. Remove from heat. Drop in the raspberries, stir, and cover pan. Allow to stand for 15 minutes. Taste and add more sugar if needed. Cool.

The traditional pairing for rhubarb is strawberries, but I prefer to combine rhubarb with raspberries. Using frozen berries makes this dish quick and easy.

9

Cookies, small treats to take along

We love to drive long distances and have crossed the country from the East Coast to the West Coast and back five times (so far). We don't plan, except for our ultimate destination, and stop to explore when something catches our eye. A few years ago we drove to Alaska and Canada's Northwest Territory to Inuvik, on the Beaufort Sear, literally at the end of the road (the Dempster highway). The trip took three months and we drove 14,000 miles. We always look for a "little treat" when driving. In fact, someone has dubbed our van "the dining-out car." The following recipe will well satisfy that momentary craving for a sweet "something." It comes from *The Pleasantville Cookbook*, published in 1894 by the Ladies of the Reading Room Association. Pleasantville, with its many restaurants, is today quite the culinary destination. The dainties are half cookie/half confection.

Brown sugar dainties

1 egg

1 cup brown sugar, firmly packed

1 teaspoon vanilla

½ cup flour

¼ teaspoon EACH baking soda and salt

1 cup coarsely chopped nuts (whatever you have on hand)

Preheat oven to 350 degrees. Stir together egg, sugar, and vanilla, then add flour, soda, and salt. Add nuts and combine thoroughly. Spoon into an 8-inch square pan and smooth the top. Bake for about 30–35 minutes or until a toothpick inserted comes out clean. Do not overbake or they will get hard. Cut into small squares and place each square in a small paper muffin cup.

Ginger treats

1½ cups flour

½ cup sugar

11 tablespoons salted butter, cut into pats

1 egg yolk

1 tablespoon water

½ cup crystallized ginger, chopped into fat little chunks

Combine flour, sugar, and butter in the bowl of a food processor and process using the metal blade. When crumbs form, add egg yolk and water and process until dough hangs together. Remove to a floured surface and knead in the ginger chunks. Cool for 30 minutes. Preheat oven to 350 degrees. Roll the pieces of dough into ¾-inch balls and place on a greased baking sheet. Flatten balls with a fork. Bake for 15–20 minutes or until light brown. Remove and cool on a rack. This recipe makes 3½ dozen.

Here is another good treat for taking along. The thicker the ginger pieces, the better the cookies will taste.

Hollenger cakes (poppy seed bars)

1 cup (2 sticks) butter, softened

1 cup light brown sugar, firmly packed

1 egg yolk

½ teaspoon vanilla extract

¼ teaspoon almond extract

2½ cups flour

1 egg white, beaten with 1 tablespoon of water

½ cup poppy seeds

Preheat oven to 350 degrees. In a large bowl or electric mixer, cream butter and sugar. Add egg yolk and two extracts, then add flour and combine thoroughly. Grease a baking sheet of 10½ x 13½ inches with a rim. Press the dough onto the sheet and roll with a lightly floured rolling pin to make an even layer. Brush with egg white and sprinkle the poppy seeds uniformly over the entire surface. (Use a dry brush to spread them properly, if necessary.) Bake for 20 minutes or until light tan and firm. Immediately cut into strips, then into diamonds. Remove the cookies from the tray while warm and cool on a rack. This recipe makes 2½ dozen, depending on size.

Bar cookies are summer favorites because they are so quick to make. This recipe is my interpretation of an old family treasure given to me by talented food photographer Richard Jacobs of Fairfield, Connecticut, who took the color photographs for this book. The sweet buttery crust blends beautifully with the poppy seed flavor. Cut into diamonds, these black-topped cookies look very appetizing when paired on a dessert plate with a scoop of ice cream or sorbet.

Jan Hagel (almond and cinnamon-sugar bar cookies)

14 tablespoons lightly salted butter

½ cup light brown sugar, firmly packed

1 teaspoon grated lemon zest

1 large egg, beaten lightly with a fork

2⅓ cups all-purpose flour

⅔ cup sliced almonds

2 tablespoons sugar, mixed with 1 teaspoon
      ground cinnamon

Preheat oven to 350 degrees. In an electric mixer, cream butter with brown sugar, zest, and 1 tablespoon of the beaten egg until the mixture is light, then stir in the flour. On a lightly buttered baking sheet with a rim, pat dough into a 14 x 10-inch rectangle, roll with a floured rolling pin to make an even layer, brush with the remaining egg, and sprinkle almonds and cinnamon sugar evenly on top. Bake for 20–25 minutes or until golden. While hot, cut into 2 x 1-inch cookies. Transfer to a rack and cool. This recipe makes 50 cookies.

Here is another bar cookie. The Dutch name Jan Hagel literally means John Hail, probably for the coarse white sugar traditionally sprinkled on top. However, I like the cookies even better when topped with sliced almonds and cinnamon sugar.

Thumbs

1½ cups flour

10 tablespoons butter

¾ cup sugar

Preheat oven to 350 degrees. Place all ingredients in the bowl of a food processor and process until a dough forms (or knead by hand). On a lightly floured surface, pat the dough into a square a little less than ½ inch thick and cut into thumb-size sticks (about 2½ inches). Bake on a buttered baking sheet for 7–10 minutes. The longer you bake them, the harder they will get. Not everyone might like cookies hard, so experiment with the first batch. This recipe makes at least 2 dozen.

This recipe is also an oldie but goodie. It comes from a handwritten Dutch cookbook and dates to the nineteenth century. In the winter, I bake these very simple, buttery cookies in a Dutch oven in the open hearth. In the summer, I make a little batch as I need them in the toaster oven and keep the rest of the dough in the refrigerator or freezer.

10

The little extras that make any occasion special

Those little extras—such as a glass of Roman punch or strawberry lemonade, a pat of herb butter on a grilled chop, homemade spicy hot tomato sauce to go with meat, or the chocolate balls with nuts and dried apricots that follow—do make an ordinary get-together noteworthy. The following recipe is simple to make; once you know how to do it, you can create your own variations.

Almond, apricot, and chocolate balls

1 cup whole almonds

8 ounces white or semisweet chocolate chips

½ cup dried apricot halves, quartered

Preheat oven to 300 degrees. Spread almonds in a single layer in a shallow pan and toast for about 12–15 minutes, stirring occasionally. Cool. Melt chocolate in the microwave; start with 30 seconds, remove, and stir; repeat for 20 seconds and then only 10 seconds and, if necessary, 10 seconds more. (Chocolate "seizes," which means it becomes granular and separates, if cooked too long or at too high a temperature.) Remove chocolate and stir in almonds and apricot pieces. Drop by heaping teaspoons onto waxed paper. Refrigerate until cool and hardened. These can be stored for 1–2 weeks in the refrigerator. This recipe makes about 24 candies.

Grandma's hot sauce

10 pounds large tomatoes

2 red hot peppers with seeds, cut into pieces

3 medium onions, peeled and cut into pieces

2 cups white or red wine vinegar

2 cups sugar

2 teaspoons salt

Wash tomatoes and cut into chunks. Put them in a large pan and slowly bring to a boil. Do not add water, but stir frequently. Boil for approximately half an hour, until very soft. Pour them through a sieve into a large bowl and rub to extract as much liquid as possible. In a blender, grind the peppers and onions very fine. Add this mixture to the tomato liquid, along with the sugar, vinegar, and salt. Stir to combine thoroughly. Cook uncovered over a low flame, so that it barely boils, for about 5 hours, stirring frequently. It will turn reddish-brown and thicken. It makes about 3 pints of pungent condiment. Pour into hot, sterilized jars or into freezer containers and cool. The hot sauce freezes well and also keeps well when refrigerated.

When there is a bumper crop of tomatoes, that is the time to make the hot sauce above. You can give small jars of the condiment as edible presents for the holidays or you might decide to reserve it all for your own family. The sauce goes particularly well with beef.

Herb butter

1 stick salted butter, softened

2 tablespoons minced parsley

2 tablespoons minced chives

2 tablespoons minced scallions

1 tablespoon minced fresh marjoram, optional

Combine butter and herbs in a small bowl. Turn out onto a piece of aluminum foil or plastic wrap. Roll into a sausage shape and twist both ends of the foil/wrap. Freeze for half an hour before using. Cut into slices and serve.

Raiding your herb garden or buying fragrant bunches of herbs at local farmers' markets to make a delicious herb butter is another way to celebrate summer. A little pat on grilled meats or vegetables will make everything taste special. Herb butter on fresh baguette slices is a treat anytime.

Peter's strawberry lemonade with lemon balm

2 (12-ounce) cans frozen pink lemonade

Juice of 2 lemons

3 sprigs of lemon balm

½ pint strawberries, cleaned and hulled

Thaw lemonade and pour into a pitcher. Dilute as indicated on the can. Add lemon juice. Remove leaves from lemon balm sprigs and combine with the strawberries in the bowl of a food processor. Finely chop mixture and add to lemonade. Stir, taste, and add more sugar, if necessary. Allow to stand for at least an hour. Add ice and serve.

Another way of making lemonade is by using the syrup recipe on page 65.

When you grow lemon balm, you always have a huge yield. I use the lemony leaves in salads, but also in this lemonade, which I serve all summer long. You can make lemonade in several ways, by pressing out lemons and combining the juice with water and sugar. The rule of thumb is to use the juice of 1 lemon for 8 ounces water. Add sugar and ice to taste. You can also use frozen lemonade or make your own syrup to have on hand all summer long. In all cases, a clean sprig of lemon balm or chopped lemon balm and strawberries are nice additions.

Lemon syrup

7 lemons

3½ cups sugar

2 cups water

With a sharp vegetable peeler, strip the yellow zest from two vigorously scrubbed lemons, avoiding the bitter, white pith. Squeeze all lemons, strain the juice, and set aside. In a saucepan, combine sugar and water and bring to a boil over medium heat, stirring constantly until sugar is dissolved. When sugar is completely dissolved and the syrup is clear, lower heat and simmer 2–3 minutes. Combine the syrup with the lemon juice and zest. Store covered at room temperature overnight. Remove zest and store the syrup in a bottle in the refrigerator. It will keep for weeks.

To use: Pour about ¼ cup of syrup into an 8-ounce glass and fill glass with plain or soda water. (Add a sprig of lemon balm.) *To make an alcoholic drink:* Mix two parts syrup with one of vodka or gin.

Roman punch

1 pint lemon sorbet
½ cup freshly squeezed orange juice
½ cup rum
½ cup seltzer

Combine all ingredients in a blender and mix thoroughly. Serve immediately or keep in the freezer.

Along or near the Hudson River still stand some of the great houses that by the mid-nineteenth century lined its shores from as far south as Manhattan's Upper West Side to as far north as Albany. Those that remain are mostly museums open to the public. Lyndhurst in Tarrytown was built in the 1840s. It was designed by architect Alexander Jackson Davis. The house changed hands several times and by 1930 it was owned by Anna Gould. After the death of her husband, Hélie de Talleyrand-Périgord, a Frenchman with the titles of prince and duke, she returned to the United States. She lived in the Plaza Hotel in New York City, but kept Lyndhurst staffed and ready for visits. The staff included a butler, who kept meticulous notes of what was served at Lyndhurst and to whom. One of the menus began with a clear chicken soup with chervil, followed by fillet of sole and roast beef. Roman punch was the palate cleanser before the next course of chicken and a dessert of coffee and bonbons concluded the meal. I adapted the recipe for the Roman punch from the Lyndhurst files as above. Use it as a palate cleanser or as a surprisingly potent summer drink.

Part II

WINTER

PREVIOUS PAGE: Snuggle by the fire in that cozy chair and decide whether to nibble on *tapas* of puffs with salmon pâté, dates stuffed with feta mousse, or horseradish and bacon spread on crackers (chapter 15—Hors d'oeuvres), or to have lunch of assorted *smørrebrød* (chapter 12—Sandwiches) and soup with curried cheese sticks (chapter 15—Hors d'oeuvres). Perhaps you feel more like a red snapper dinner with a glass of white wine, but no matter what meal you choose, there will be a sweet ending of baked treats such as a puff pastry stick filled with almond paste, cherry *kuchen* (chapter 18—Desserts) and spiced *speculaas* cookies or Bourbon balls (chapter 19—Cookies). Battenfeld's hybrid Anemones are grown from September to May in Red Hook, New York.

PHOTO: *Richard Jacobs*; FOOD STYLING: *Peter G. Rose*

Introduction

Winters in the Hudson Valley can be mild, but there are always some cold months. Comforting, warming foods are just what are called for in times when the temperature slips below 32 degrees. Those are the kind of seasonal dishes, some old, some new, you will find in this Winter Pleasures section. And pleasures they are indeed. Brisk winter walks, ice skating on the valley's many lakes or reservoirs, sledding down the hills, or cross-country skiing in the woods—all these activities help work up an appetite. The Catskill mountain range that borders the Hudson Valley has two well-known ski areas at Windham Mountain (Ski Windham) in the north and Belleayre Mountain in Highmount in its heart. Both offer a wide range of activities.

The Hudson Valley can boast of famous chefs and many fine restaurants. Veteran chef John Novi of the DuPuy Canal House in High Falls, Peter Kelly with his new restaurant X20 Xaviar's on the Hudson on the pier in Yonkers (with a stunning view of the river), and John Barber of Blue Hill at Stone Barns in Pocantico Hills are only a few of the large Hudson Valley culinary group making an effort to introduce new tastes and new products, but also to support local farmers. In addition, another source of pride for the valley is the Culinary Institute of America in Hyde Park. Visiting the institute's restaurants, where the students work as servers and chefs, is a most interesting and enjoyable culinary adventure.

Winter

A swirling snowstorm surrounds our house as I am writing this and I am glad to be home. Home is what this section is all about. Home, where you can make a sturdy breakfast of pancakes and sausage, prepare a leisurely lunch for a snow(y) day, cook up a big pot of soup when it is cold outside, or put together a simple main meal with winter vegetables and a tempting dessert. Afterwards, you can nestle in by the fire with a plate of cookies and sigh with pleasure.

The recipes in this section are a mixture of new and old, some even old-fashioned, but all make dishes that please. Most incorporate our local produce, but to exclude all the foods from supermarkets would be unrealistic and unnecessary, although we all make an effort to support our Hudson Valley farmers. Winter farm markets are now coming into fashion and need our backing. Pat Imbimbo, who calls himself "owner, farmer, beekeeper, and janitor" of New England Farms in Granville, has organized such a winter farm in my town of Lewisboro at the edge of the Hudson Valley Heritage area. Familiar names and products such as Bread Alone from Boiceville or Migliorelli's from Tivoli are represented here. Some farmers drive hours to bring their products to market. Fortunately, they find local support and these farm markets have become gathering places where you can meet and greet neighbors.

Living in our beautiful valley with its centuries-old history is a pleasure; visiting it is a joy. But, for now, put on your slippers, snuggle by the fire, and enjoy good food.

11

Breakfast foods that make a difference

On winter weekdays when you have to allow extra minutes for scraping the car, there is little time for a formal breakfast, so taking a breakfast cookie along might be a good solution. The other four recipes in this chapter are meant for the more leisurely occasions on the weekend.

If you have not yet discovered the Smoke House of the Catskills in Saugerties, I suggest you stop the next time you are in that area. It is located just off the New York State Thruway on Route 212. It is a *Deutsche Metzgerei* (German butcher shop) with authentic German specialty meats and other German products. We are particularly fond of their Polish kielbasa, clearly made with wholesome ingredients, but other sausages are very good as well and so is the carefully trimmed meat. I use the kielbasa Dutch-style in the pancakes on page 73, which would serve as a meal in the Netherlands. We ate them in a restaurant where the rule was that if you could eat the whole pancake, you got a second one free. Few people asked for more, so I assure you that this makes a hearty breakfast. Traditionally, these pancakes are at least 12 inches in diameter, but a 9-inch omelet pan makes a more manageable breakfast size. The Polish kielbasa is fully cooked. The batter can be made the night before and kept in the refrigerator.

Breakfast cookies

12 tablespoons butter

1¼ cup dark brown sugar, lightly packed

1 egg

2¼ cups all-purpose flour

1 teaspoon baking soda

1¼ cup oats

½ teaspoon salt

1 teaspoon cinnamon

½ teaspoon cardamom

¼ teaspoon EACH cloves, nutmeg

1 cup trail mix (see below)

1 cup raisins

Cream butter and sugar; add egg and combine. In a separate bowl stir together the flour, baking soda, oats, salt, cinnamon, cardamom, cloves, and nutmeg. Add to the butter mixture and combine, then stir in trail mix and raisins. Chill the dough for 30 minutes. Preheat the oven to 350 degrees. Butter a baking sheet. Shape the dough into 8 patties as for hamburgers and flatten to about 3 inches in diameter and ¾ inch thick. Bake for 20–25 minutes. Cool on a rack and when cooled store in an air-tight container. This recipe makes 8 breakfast cookies.

Randell Dodge is one of the participants in our town's winter market with the products from her organic Red Barn Bakery. She came up with the idea of breakfast cookies that are a meal in themselves and nicely replace muffins or doughnuts for a "grab 'n go" start of the day. The cookies have the added advantage that they stay fresh in an airtight box for about a week. I used Nantucket Trail Mix as a short cut here. It contains raw almonds, raw cashews, pepitas, pecans, raw sunflower seed, diced mango, pineapple, golden raisins, and cranberries. Any similar mixture may be used.

Breakfast pancakes with kielbasa sausage

1 package (¼ ounce) active dry yeast

½ cup warm water (100–110 dregrees)

½ teaspoon sugar

3 cups flour

2 eggs

3 cups milk

1 teaspoon salt

Sliced kielbasa, fully cooked, about 8 slices per pancake

1 tablespoon EACH vegetable oil and butter for frying each pancake

In a small bowl, pour the water, sprinkle on the yeast, and top with sugar. Allow to stand a few minutes, stir, and set aside in a warm place for 5–10 minutes or until bubbly. In a large bowl or an electric mixer, stir together flour, prepared yeast mixture, and eggs, slowly adding milk to make a smooth batter without lumps. Cover and allow to rise for about 1½ hours. (Or store in a jar in the refrigerator overnight and use in the morning.) In an omelet pan, heat oil and butter until butter has melted. Pour in about ½ cup of the batter and tilt pan to cover the bottom. Drop in the sausage slices in a neat pattern and cook the pancake until browned on the bottom. Carefully turn over and brown the other side. Check to make sure it is cooked through, remove to a plate, and serve with syrup.

If you prefer an apple pancake rather than the sausage, peel and quarter an apple, cut each quarter into thin slices, and add 8 slices to the pancake in the way you would add the sausage.

Canadian bacon with apples

Use 1 apple per person; peel whole apple, core, and cut across into thick slices

½ teaspoon cinnamon and 1 teaspoon sugar for each apple, optional

2 or more slices of Canadian bacon per person

Vegetable oil or butter for frying

In a large frying pan, heat some oil and add apple slices in a single layer. Sprinkle with cinnamon and sugar, if used. Over medium heat, fry apple slices until light brown on the bottom, turn over, and fry other side. When done, add a dash of water to the pan, cover, and set aside off the heat. In another frying pan, heat a little oil and briefly fry bacon on both sides over low heat, just until heated through (it is fully cooked already). Serve apple slices topped with bacon with the hot toast and jam.

Fried apples pair well with any pork product, but they are particularly nice for breakfast served with lean Canadian bacon and hot toast with strawberry jam.

Herbed omelet with chanterelles

4 ounces chanterelles mushrooms

3½ tablespoon butter, divided

Salt and white (if you have it) pepper to taste

3 eggs

¼ teaspoon salt

2 tablespoons milk

2 scallions, minced

1 tablespoon EACH minced parsley and minced celery leaves

Carefully wash chanterelles under running water. Cut into pieces if they are big. Leave little ones whole. Blot dry with paper towels. In a small frying pan, melt 1½ tablespoons of butter and quickly fry the mushrooms for a few minutes. Season with salt and pepper; cover, and set aside in a warm place. In a bowl, combine eggs, salt, and milk, and beat with a whisk until frothy. Add the scallions, parsley, and celery and beat for 1 minute more. In a 10-inch omelet pan (see note), melt 2 tablespoons butter. Pour the egg mixture into the pan and cook over low heat. When omelet is cooked through, use a slotted spoon to place chanterelles on one half, fold over the other half, and slide onto a warm plate. Cut in half to serve two. Accompany with buttered toast or English muffins. *Note:* I suggest using a larger pan than usual. This makes the omelet thinner and less spongy, so that it will not overpower the flavor of the delicate mushrooms.

There is only a brief period in the fall when chanterelles are available, so make the best of it. If you are accustomed to searching for mushrooms and are absolutely certain about what to pick, you know that finding chanterelles under oak brush where they like to grow is akin to finding gold. This omelet is an extravagant treat for two.

Honey muffins

½ cup Hudson Valley honey

½ cup orange juice

½ cup butter, melted and cooled

2 eggs, beaten lightly with a fork

1 teaspoon vanilla

2 cups of flour

¼ cup sugar

2 teaspoons baking powder

1 teaspoon baking soda

½ teaspoon salt

Preheat oven to 375 degrees. In a small bowl, combine honey, orange juice, butter, eggs, and vanilla; mix well. Combine flour, sugar, baking powder, baking soda, and salt in a mixing bowl. Stir liquid mixture into dry ingredients until well blended. Line muffin cups with paper inserts and spoon batter into each cup about two-thirds full. Bake for 15–20 minutes or until golden. This recipe makes 12 perfect muffins.

Since there is an abundance of local honey available in the Hudson Valley, use it to best advantage in these fragrant, golden muffins.

12

Sandwiches

My mother told me that if you learn how to make a white sauce, you'll never go hungry because there are so many things you can do with it. I use it in the first sandwich recipe to make a chicken and mushroom ragoût that can be served over rice for lunch or as a first course for dinner on toast, a toasted English muffin, or in a puff pastry shell. Yes, it is a version of what used to be called Chicken à la King, usually followed by nose-wrinkling because it did not have the reputation of being a tasty dish. I think you'll agree with me when you make it according to the following recipe that that reputation is undeserved.

It might surprise you that there is a Danish Home for the Aged in the Hudson Valley, but the area has a large variety of ethnic groups including African Americans, Dutch, English, French, Germans, Hispanics, Hungarians, Irish, Italians, Poles, and Russians, and many more as well as the Danes. The building and grounds, hidden in the woods in Croton-on-Hudson, were purchased by the Benevolent Society "Danmark" in 1954. The society, founded on March 18, 1903, established a Danish home for the aged in Brooklyn until it was moved to its present country location. This is a cheerful place, not at all an institution. Residents have their own rooms, furnished with their own possessions if they wish, and their own bathrooms. They are lovingly cared for by the staff and Danish customs are maintained in all ways possible, particularly at the holidays and in the cuisine.

A favorite evening meal there is *smørrebrød*. The word means "buttered bread," open-faced sandwiches generously topped with

whatever pleases you. Traditionally, the *smørrebrød* is accompanied by a small glass of *akvavit* and an ice-cold Carlsberg beer. With or without those drinks, *smørrebrød* make an appealing Sunday lunch that can easily be made with American ingredients.

Chicken and mushroom ragoût on toast

1 tablespoon vegetable oil

10 ounces sliced mushrooms, rinsed and dried

2 tablespoons EACH chopped scallions and parsley

6 tablespoons butter

6 tablespoons flour

1½ cup milk or half-and-half

1–1½ cups of cooked chicken (or leftover turkey), diced

½ teaspoon salt and ¼ teaspoon freshly ground (preferably white) pepper

NOTE:
When making a flour and butter (white) sauce, cook the sauce for a few minutes to remove the raw flour taste.

In a frying pan, heat oil and add mushrooms, scallions, and parsley. Cook while stirring until mushrooms are browned on both sides. Remove and set aside. In a saucepan, melt butter. When melted, add flour and stir with a whisk until combined. Reduce heat, slowly add the milk or half-and-half, and whisk to make a smooth sauce. Cook while stirring for 2 minutes. This is important because the cooking removes the raw flour taste. Add mushrooms with liquid, if any, and chicken; stir to combine. Taste, and season with salt and pepper. Serve as suggested on page 77.

Danish *smørrebrød* (open-faced sandwich) with Italian salad

Smørrebrød

Butter

Dark bread, thinly sliced

Sliced ham

Large red onion, cut into thick slices and

separated into rings

Evenly butter bread slices, top with ham, place a red onion ring on the ham, and heap the salad (below) in the ring. These sandwiches are traditionally eaten with knife and fork.

Italian salad

2 large carrots, peeled and diced

¾ cup tiny frozen peas

10 thin asparagus, chopped

3 tablespoons peach juice (from a can of peaches)

or a little sugar, optional

Mayonnaise

Salt and pepper to taste

In a small saucepan, cook carrots with water to cover. When they have softened somewhat, add peas and asparagus and cook for just a few more minutes until done to your liking. Drain, if necessary, and cool. In a small bowl, combine the vegetables with enough mayonnaise to bind and add the peach juice, if desired. Season to taste with salt and freshly ground pepper. Use the salad as a garnish as described above.

The "buttered bread," or open-faced sandwiches can be topped with whatever you like. At the Croton-on-Hudson Danish Home for the Aged, the traditional thinly sliced sour rye bread has toppings of Harvarti cheese with rosettes of parsley; liver pâté decorated with strips of cooked beet; roast beef topped with pickle slices or fried onions; and ham combined with hard-boiled egg slices or "Italian salad." Choose three or four different toppings—leftovers from dinner can be used, such as meat, seafood, or cooked vegetables. Find garnishes that complement each other in taste and texture. Arrange everything attractively and serve on a platter. The smørrebrod can be made several hours ahead and refrigerated.

Italian salad was one of the garnishes used when I visited. Everywhere else this kind of salad is called "Russian salad." This recipe has an unusual ingredient, peach syrup (from a can of peaches), which gives it a sweet flavor, but, lacking peach juice, you can add a little sugar to the mayonnaise.

Donna's egg salads

Egg salad

6 hard-boiled eggs, finely diced
1/4–1/3 cup mayonnaise

… with green olives and fennel

2 tablespoons chopped green pimento-filled olives
2 tablespoons finely chopped fennel (or the feathery fronds)

… with black olives and red pepper

2 tablespoons chopped black olives
2 tablespoons minced red pepper
substitute 1/4–1/3 cup *garlic* mayonnaise

… with lox and dill

2–3 tablespoons finely diced lox
2 tablespoons minced dill

… with ham and pineapple

3 tablespoons finely diced ham
2–3 tablespoons finely diced pineapple
1/2 teaspoon curry powder

… with shrimp and water chestnuts

About 1/3 pound cooked shrimp, chopped
3 tablespoons water chestnuts, chopped
1–2 teaspoons soy sauce

It is fun to "talk food" with your friends, and on just such an occasion, my friend Donna Barnes gave me these suggestions for egg salads. They are particularly handy when you are faced with a basket of colored hard-boiled eggs after Easter. Just combine the ingredients and serve on your favorite bread.

Portobello mushroom sandwich

1 large portobello mushroom cap, stem removed, rinsed, and drained

Vegetable oil

1 small onion, peeled, cut in half and crosswise into thin slices

4 ½-inch thick tomato slices

1 large handful fresh (baby) spinach leaves, washed

1–2 roasted peppers (from a jar), drained

Sliced mozzarella cheese for topping

2 slices good whole wheat, or whole grain bread, toasted

Brush mushroom cap with vegetable oil, season with salt and pepper, and grill in a toaster oven (gill-side up) until soft and pliable, about 7–10 minutes. In the meantime, heat a tablespoon of oil in a small skillet, fry onion slices until they are limp, and add the tomatoes. Cook tomato slices on both sides for about 4 minutes. Add the spinach, cover pan, and cook for 2 minutes more, just to wilt the vegetable. To assemble: On a large plate, place the two toasted bread slices. Cut the mushroom cap in half and put each half on a slice of bread. Top with peppers, onion, tomato, and spinach and cover with sliced mozzarella. Run under the broiler, long enough to melt the cheese. Serve immediately as suggested below.

This recipe was given to me by the kitchen of the Kit 'n Caboodle Restaurant in Mount Kisco, now, alas, gone. The sandwich is filling enough to be dinner, especially if you accompany it with a cup of cucumber or celery root soup. If you prefer, instead of soup, add a dessert such as a slice of cherry kuchen or a helping of the apple-nut surprise.

Vegetable Reuben sandwich

2 tablespoons olive oil

1 EACH yellow and green squash, sliced crosswise, cut large slices in half

10 ounces sliced mushrooms, rinsed and dried

1 medium onion, thinly sliced and separated into rings

1 EACH red and green pepper, core and seeds removed, diced

Salt and freshly ground pepper

4 sprigs fresh dill, chopped

8 basil leaves, sliced

Rye bread

Thousand Island dressing

Sauerkraut (see note)

Swiss cheese slices

In a large frying pan, heat oil, then add squash, mushrooms, onion, and peppers and cook while stirring occasionally. Cook until barely done. Add salt and pepper and mix in the herbs. Stir to combine, cool, and refrigerate. This mixture can be kept in the refrigerator for several days.

To assemble a sandwich

Toast two slices of rye bread. In the microwave, heat a small portion of the vegetable mixture and combine it with a few tablespoons of sauerkraut. Spread one slice of the toast with Thousand Island dressing; add the warm vegetables/sauerkraut mixture, and top with cheese. Place back in the microwave to melt cheese, top with the second slice of toast, and serve (or serve the sandwich open-faced). The vegetable mixture is enough for 6–8 sandwiches.

NOTE:

Commercial sauerkraut can be very sour. If so, rinse before using and cook for 15 minutes on low heat in a cup of fruity white wine. The Smokehouse of the Catskills sells canned wine-cooked mild German sauerkraut that is very good.

Some years ago, we removed the mast from our sailboat Pot Luck and took her through the thirty-five locks of the Erie Canal all the way to North Tonawanda, from where you can access the Great Lakes. This is called "locking through" in canal speak. We did not go to the lakes—just turned around in Tonawanda and came back. The Erie Canal truly is—as has been said—New York State's best kept secret and an exciting extension of the Hudson River. It was a glorious trip; we loved it so much that we did it again the next summer. One day a little boy came up to our boat and studied her for the longest time and finally asked: "Did this used to be a yacht?" Without her mast Pot Luck looks decidedly odd, but we don't mind. It is a small sacrifice to make in order to see the beautiful Erie Canal.

On that second trip, we met Karen and Larry Lee, who were on their way to take their boat to California. Many of the boaters on the canal are going from the Midwest to Florida and (way) beyond. It makes the trip even more enjoyable to meet all these adventurous folks. We traveled with the Lees all the way back to Croton-on-Hudson, home port for our boat, docking in various towns along the way and spending many a pleasant evening eating some of the recipes you find here and listening to the various dockside concerts offered during the summer. We were together in Waterford when all the lights went off in the Northeast due to a gigantic power failure. Passers-by gave us envious glances as we were sitting by candlelight (as usual) as cozy as can be. One of them called out: "You guys really know how to live!"

A favorite stop on both trips was Little Falls, once known for its important cheese market—so important that cheese prices set there were the base for markets in the rest of the country. Now it is a fun town to go antiquing and shopping at Canal Place, a huge renovated industrial building converted into shops. For breakfast, we always visit the Ann Street Restaurant & Deli, within easy walking distance from the dock and canal-side park. Grace Klutschkowski, the owner at the time, gave me the recipe on page 84 for one of their most popular sandwiches, and it's easy to understand why they are so popular when you taste one. The delicious vegetable mixture with or without sauerkraut or cheese also makes a very nice accompaniment to a plain grilled or fried chicken breast.

13

Salads

Most winter vegetables can be made into salads, which is a handy way of dealing with leftovers. Particularly good are the four used here, but be creative with what is available. Try a shelled bean salad of cranberry beans, canned white beans, or chick peas with finely cut onion, cucumber, and red pepper, and a vinaigrette dressing. Steamed broccoli needs little more than a tart lemon dressing. Red or green cabbage can be made into coleslaw. Try the seventeenth-century Dutch way: thinly cut cabbage and mix with a dressing of melted butter and vinegar with a little sugar, salt, and pepper. Be sure to keep it at room temperature or the butter will congeal.

The first salad can be made with either leftover beets or canned ones. The currants add extra tang and a slight chewiness to the mixture, while the celery adds crunch.

Beet salad with celery and currants

2 cans sliced beets, drained, or an equivalent amount of
cooked beets (about 3 cups) cut into sticks

3 or 4 inner celery stalks with greens, finely chopped

4 tablespoon currants

Salt and freshly ground pepper

Vinaigrette

In a salad bowl, combine all ingredients and allow to marinate for 1 hour
before serving.

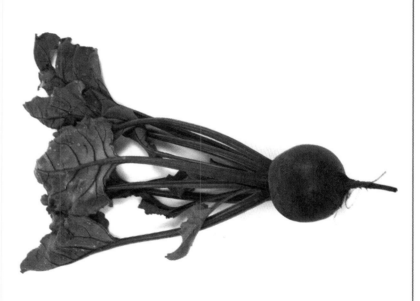

Belgian endive salad with orange

3 Belgian endives

1 orange

⅓ cup vinegar, preferable white Balsamic

¼ cup olive oil

Half a ripe banana

Sugar, salt, and freshly ground pepper

Cut a thin slice from the ends of the endives and slice them into ¾-inch pieces. Peel the orange and cut between segments to eliminate any skin. Cut each piece in half. In a medium bowl, mix endive and orange pieces, including any juice resulting from cutting the oranges. In a small bowl, mash the banana half and combine with the vinegar and oil. Season the dressing with a small teaspoon of sugar, salt, and pepper. Pour onto the endive mixture and combine thoroughly. Serve or keep refrigerated for up to 24 hours.

NOTE:
For salads, vegetables or pasta should be cooked until barely done, because the dressing will further soften them.

This recipe comes from the Netherlands, where Belgian endive is far more popular than it is here. Our hostess, Jannie Visser of Zevenhuizen, near the cheese town of Gouda, gave me the recipe. It is an easy salad, which can be made ahead.

Brussels sprouts salad

1 pound Brussels sprouts, outer leaves removed and bottom

cut or 1 (10-ounce) package frozen Brussels sprouts,

thawed

⅓ cup minced parsley

15 walnut halves

1 or 2 scallions, minced

Vinaigrette

Salt and freshly ground pepper

Briefly cook the Brussels sprouts in ⅓ cup water until barely done. Drain and spoon into a bowl and add the remaining ingredients and the vinaigrette dressing while the sprouts are still warm. Cool and serve.

Brussels sprouts are a quintessential winter vegetable found at any of the valley's fall farmers' markets. Some are still on the stalk and appear quite decorative when displayed in a basket in the kitchen until ready to use. You can use fresh or frozen sprouts for this salad.

Cauliflower salad with cumin dressing

1 cauliflower, outer leaves and core removed and separated
   into 2-inch florets (about 3 cups)

3 tablespoons olive or vegetable oil

1 medium shallot, or onion, chopped

1 teaspoon ground cumin

⅓ cup red wine vinegar

Salt, freshly ground pepper, and sugar to taste

2 tablespoons minced parsley

Steam the cauliflower until barely done. In a frying pan, heat oil and cook shallot or onion until translucent, but not brown. Stir in cumin and cook 1 minute more, then add vinegar. Season with salt, pepper, and sugar; taste and adjust seasoning, if necessary. Place the cauliflower in a glass bowl and pour warm dressing over it. Toss lightly to combine. Allow to cool. Stir in parsley before serving.

For salads, all vegetables should be cooked until barely done because dressings further soften them. The cumin in the dressing complements the cabbage flavor. You will be surprised how good this is.

Donna's winter salad

Baby spinach, or other greens

2 navel oranges, carefully peeled and white pith removed,
  sliced into thin rounds

Ground cinnamon

Half of 1 red onion, thinly sliced

5 large radishes, thinly sliced

Orange vinaigrette (see chapter 20)

Pomegranate seeds or golden raisins

On a round platter, make a bed of greens. On top of the greens, arrange concentric circles of orange slices, dust lightly with cinnamon, then make circles of onion and radish slices. Dress the salad with the orange vinaigrette and sprinkle with the pomegranate seeds or raisins.

Here is another recipe from my friend Donna Barnes that makes a beautiful vegetable dish for a winter meal of ham or pork. It is fresh and tangy—a bit of spring in the heart of winter.

14

Soups, hot
for a cold winter's day

Soups are versatile: they can be paired with a sandwich for lunch, served as a first course for dinner, or they can be a meal in themselves. Here are five choices made with winter vegetables. You decide how to serve them—or you might consider copying an interesting idea from the Culinary Institute of America in Hyde Park and present a trio of soups. As they are eating, ask your friends to rate them in the order of their preference; everybody has fun and the lineups frequently differ.

Cauliflower soup

1 cauliflower

4 tablespoons butter

4 tablespoons flour

4 cups of cooking water

1 cup half-and-half, optional

Salt and freshly ground pepper

Ground nutmeg to taste

Remove outer leaves of the cauliflower. Cut in half and remove the white core. In a large pan, cook cauliflower pieces with salted water to barely cover until very soft. Drain and save the cooking water. With a potato masher, coarsely mash cauliflower pieces. Remove to a bowl and set aside. In the pan, melt the butter, add flour, and stir with a whisk until combined. Slowly, on low heat, add the cooking water to make a cream soup, then add the half-and-half. Discard the rest of the water as necessary. Add the cauliflower to the pan and stir to combine. Taste and adjust seasoning with salt, pepper, and nutmeg to taste.

Celery root soup

2 tablespoons vegetable oil

1 medium celery root, peeled and finely diced (about 2 cups)

2 tablespoons scallions

3 tablespoons flour

4 cups beef broth (see below)

3 inner celery stalks with greens, minced (about ¾ cup)

Salt and freshly ground pepper

Dry sherry, preferably Manzanilla, optional

In a large saucepan, heat oil and cook the diced celery root over low heat until light brown and done, about 10 minutes. Add scallions and sprinkle with flour and stir to combine. Slowly whisk in the broth. Add the minced celery stalks and cook for 10 minutes more. Season with salt and pepper to taste. Add a teaspoon (or more) of sherry to each serving, if desired. This makes a nice light (and warming) starter for a meat-and-potatoes dinner.

Celery root is a vegetable not frequently used in most households, yet it is quite flavorful and together with some green celery makes a tasty winter soup. Good beef broth is essential. You can certainly use commercial broth, but refresh it by simmering it for 20 minutes with 2 bay leaves, 1 clove, a celery stalk cut into three pieces, a carrot cut into sticks, 2 slices of onion, and about ¼ cup dry red or white wine. Strain and measure; if needed, add water to make the necessary 4 cups. The idea for refreshing commercial broth I owe to my treasured food-friend Stephen Schmidt.

Cucumber soup with radishes

2 tablespoons vegetable oil

1 medium onion, peeled and finely chopped

2 cucumbers, cut in half, seeds removed, and cut into
chunks

⅓ cup minced parsley

4 cups beef broth (see my remarks on refreshing commercial
broth at the end of the previous recipe)

1 cup half-and-half or whole milk

¼ teaspoon freshly ground (preferably white) pepper

6–8 radishes, finely diced (about ½ cup)

Grated Gouda, Parano, Old Amsterdam, or Parmesan cheese

In a large saucepan, heat oil and cook onion and cucumber pieces over low heat until onion is translucent and cucumber softened. Add the parsley and cook for 1 minute more. Stir in the broth and half-and-half or milk. Use an immersion blender or regular blender to puree the mixture. It will foam, but by stirring the bubbles will disappear. Reheat and add pepper and diced radishes. Taste and adjust seasonings, as necessary. Add a heaping tablespoon of grated cheese to each serving.

While cucumbers and radishes are of course not winter vegetables, they are so readily available that I am using them, especially because with its light green color and red/white garnish the soup seems perfect for the holiday season. The flavor is subtle, but the radish gives it crunch and a slightly peppery taste. The grated cheese adds body to this low-calorie soup.

Mustard soup

3 tablespoons butter

1 large shallot, peeled and finely chopped

3 tablespoons flour

4 cups chicken broth—the better the broth, the better the

soup

3 tablespoons Dijon grainy mustard

1 cup EACH milk and half-and-half

Salt and freshly ground pepper

1/4–1/2 teaspoon turmeric for color

In a large saucepan with a heavy bottom, melt butter, add the shallot, and sprinkle on the flour. Cook, while stirring, until lightly browned. Then whisk in the chicken stock and mustard and simmer for half an hour. Add milk and half-and-half and simmer for a few more minutes. Taste and adjust seasonings with more mustard, salt, and freshly ground pepper. Stir in the turmeric to improve the color, if necessary.

For years, mustard soup has been a favorite with family and friends. The fun in making it is that you can vary the flavor with different mustards. Try it first with a grainy Dijon as in the recipe above, then create your own version using different mustard choices. Particularly good is a coarse Dutch mustard, called Zaanse mosterd, available in Dutch specialty stores. Of course any of the Hudson Valley mustards add variety as well. Mustard gets its name from the fact that it originally was made from mustard seeds and must (freshly pressed grape juice not yet fermented into wine.). It is prepared from either Brassica juncea (brown/black) or Brassica hirta (white/blond) seeds and sometimes from a combination of both.

Potato soup with white wine

2 pounds Idaho or Yukon Gold potatoes, peeled

1 medium onion, peeled

4 medium carrots, scraped

4 tablespoons butter

1/3 cup plus 1 tablespoon all-purpose flour

6 cups vegetable or chicken broth

1 cup dry white wine

1/4 teaspoon ground mace

Salt and freshly ground pepper

4 tablespoons minced parsley

2 tablespoons minced celery leaves, if available

NOTE:
Vegetable cooking-water can be the base for a soup.

Cut potatoes crosswise into thin coins. Finely chop the onion and cut carrots into thin slices. Set aside. Melt butter in a large saucepan, use a whisk to stir in the flour, and allow flour to color slightly. Gradually add broth. Stir vigorously to create a smooth sauce. Stir in the white wine and add potatoes, carrots, onion, and mace. Bring to a boil and reduce heat to simmer. Cook until everything is well done, about 20 minutes or so. Taste and season the soup with salt, pepper, and the fresh herbs. Allow to simmer for just a few minutes more. If you prefer a smooth soup, use an immersion blender or regular blender to puree it, but that is not necessary.

This soup is heavier and can be eaten as a meal, perhaps on a day when you have a nice dessert on hand. The wine is essential to the good taste of the soup and is a nice way to use up leftover wine. Please do not use cooking wine—it is generally sour and bitter.

15

Hors d'oeuvres or anytime snacks

I nvite your friends for a relaxing time by the fire on a late Sunday afternoon and serve drinks and substantial hors d'oeuvres or tapas. All of the following choices can be made ahead and offer interesting variety. The curried cheese sticks are a handy standby for any occasion and keep well in an airtight box. Simply refresh the sticks by reheating them for a few minutes in a (toaster) oven set at 300 degrees and they are ready to serve.

Curried cheese sticks

1 package puff pastry sheets (I use Pepperidge Farm brand)

1 egg, beaten with 1 tablespoon of water

Mild curry powder

Finely grated aged cheese, Parmesan, Old Amsterdam,

or Parano

Remove one pastry sheet from the package and wrap the other in plastic wrap and freeze for another use. Thaw on the counter according to package instructions (40 minutes). Preheat oven to 400 degrees. Unfold the sheet and you will see three folds; leave intact and place the sheet with the wide side toward you on the counter. Brush all over with egg. Sprinkle LIGHTLY with curry powder. Sprinkle heavily with finely grated cheese. Cut the sheet into three parts along the folds. Use a flat, clean ruler, start on top, press down, and cut across into sticks of ¾ inch wide. (The ruler helps the topping to adhere.) Remove sticks to a buttered baking sheet and bake for 12–15 minutes or until puffed and golden. Cool and store in an airtight box.

Dates stuffed with feta mousse and wrapped in bacon

7 slices bacon

1 egg white

3 ounces feta, very finely crumbled

14 pitted dates

Fry bacon until most of the grease is rendered and rashers are light brown and limp. Drain on paper towels and cool. Preheat oven to 325 degrees. Beat the egg white until soft peaks start to form, then add the crumbled feta a little at a time so that all is incorporated. Slit the dates lengthwise. Use a small spoon to fill each with the feta mousse. Cut the bacon slices in half and wrap a half slice around each date and secure with a toothpick. Place in one layer in an ovenproof dish and bake for 20 minutes or until filling is cooked. Serve two per person on a small plate. (They'll come back for more!)

Some fifteen years ago, we stayed in St. Louis for a while, at a time when tapas were still relatively new to the American culinary scene. I was given the recipe above by Chef Steve Komorek of a small restaurant named Piccolo and have used it ever since. Tapas restaurants now abound in the Hudson Valley from Larchmont or White Plains to Rhinebeck and Saugerties and many towns in between. With the five recipes in this hors d'oeuvres section you can make a tasty tapas menu. Though not Spanish in flavor, it will represent the spirit of these "small plates."

In this recipe, prepare the dates ahead and bake them half an hour before your guests arrive. Leave the dates in the turned-off, cooling oven until ready to serve.

Horseradish and bacon spread

4 to 6 slices bacon, depending on size

8 ounces cream cheese, softened

1 tablespoon prepared hot horseradish

Salt, pepper, and sugar

A few tablespoons of milk

Fry bacon until golden and crisp. Drain on paper towels, wipe off any remaining grease, and finely crumble slices. In a small bowl, combine cream cheese, horseradish, crumbled bacon, and a little milk to make a soft, spreading consistency. Adjust seasonings with salt, pepper, perhaps a dash of sugar, and more horseradish to taste. Chill for at least an hour. Serve with crackers. This spread is at its best when served on the day it is made.

Use the outstanding bacon from Mountain Products in LaGrangeville or your own favorite brand for the previous recipe as well as for the horseradish bacon spread. Another recipe that is so simple and so good!

Mushroom tart

2 tablespoons vegetable oil

1 cup thinly sliced sweet onion, cut into half-circles and
separated

10 ounces wild or domestic mushrooms (see below), cleaned

2 tablespoons parsley, minced, divided

Salt and freshly ground pepper, to taste

1 pie crust (see below), thawed

1½ cups finely grated Gouda or Fontina cheese

½ cup crumbled feta cheese, or more to taste

In a frying pan, heat oil, reduce heat, and slowly cook onion until browned
and caramelized. Remove and set aside. Add the mushrooms and 1 tablespoon of
parsley to the pan and over medium heat quickly brown the mushrooms. Remove
from heat. Season with salt and pepper. On a lightly floured counter, unroll the pie
crust and place on a buttered baking sheet. Pat down an even layer of the grated

*For the mushroom tart above, you can use a commercial pie crust. I favor
the rolled-up crusts from Pillsbury, which you can find in the dairy section
of the supermarket.*

*There is even a Hudson Valley connection between mushrooms from all
around the world and our area. Hans Johansson of Katonah is a distribu-
tor of such mushrooms and delights in the romance of his product. In his
native Sweden, children are taken on walks in the woods and encouraged
to identify the trees, plants, and mushrooms they encounter. That early
education started his interest. Twenty-five years ago it became his business,
at a time "when people had only just heard about shiitake." For this recipe,
use a mixture of wild mushrooms or just sliced white mushrooms, according
to your inclination.*

cheese, leaving a 1½-inch plain border all around. Top the cheese layer first with the onions and then with the mushrooms. Fold dough border up all around the rim and slightly over filling and bake for 40 minutes in the lower half of the oven or until the crust is brown. Remove, sprinkle with feta and parsley, and return to oven for 3 minutes (turn oven off). Cut into 8 wedges and serve warm or at room temperature. Easy and delicious!

Puffs with salmon pâté

Puffs

1 cup water

6 tablespoons butter

¼ teaspoon salt

1 cup all-purpose flour or bread flour

3 large or 4 medium eggs

Preheat oven to 450 degrees. In a medium saucepan, bring water, butter, and salt to a boil. Remove from heat. Stir in flour all at once and beat with an electric hand mixer (or transfer to the bowl of an electric mixer) until mixture leaves the side of the pan. Cool for a few minutes; then add eggs one at a time, beating well after each addition until the mixture is smooth and glossy. Using 2 tablespoons, mound into 1-inch balls onto a greased baking sheet. Bake 15 minutes, reduce oven to 350 degrees, and bake for 20–30 minutes or until puffs are golden and dry. Cool on racks. Open and fill with the following.

Salmon pâté

8 ounces smoked salmon, finely chopped

1/3 cup EACH mayonnaise and
　　reduced-fat sour cream

3 scallions, finely chopped

2 heaping tablespoons nonpareil (tiny)
　　capers or large chopped capers

Lots of coarsely ground fresh pepper and salt
　　as necessary (see note)

NOTE:

Taste before seasoning because commercial smoked salmon is very salty.

In a small bowl, combine ingredients and spoon into puffs. This recipe makes
30. Leftover filling, if any, can be served with crackers.

*Recipes for cream puffs appeared already in the sixteenth century in French
and English cookbooks; however, they were served by themselves, not filled.
Fillings did not appear in cookbooks until the nineteenth century. Nowadays
we know that cream puffs are not only for cream, but can be very effectively
used for hors d'oeuvres. They make fine finger food and can be filled with
cheese butters, shrimp or chicken salad, or the salmon pâté above. I learned
this recipe from John Chatellier in Millbrook, who sold us our small (no
bigger than a shoebox) Ol' Ruff smoker, which we use to smoke chunks of
salmon on the patio during the summer and also in the winter. We took it
along on our boat trips on the Erie Canal and smoked fish or pork chops
dockside; we always drew a crowd of interested onlookers.*

16

Simple main courses

The next five recipes are warming dishes for wintertime. All five are easy to make and offer a variety of flavors. Citrus fruits are our winter delight. Used in abundance here in a bed of lemons to bake the fish and in the zest used in the lemon butter mixture, they are shown off to their best advantage.

Lemons were probably first cultivated in India, although pinpointing their initial popularity in Europe is difficult—they could have been introduced by crusaders returning from the Middle East. History confuses lemons, limes, and citrons, so exact dates and places are debatable. Most historians agree that inhabitants of Spain and North Africa used lemons around 1000 A.D.; more ancient Roman mosaics appear to depict lemons as early as the second or third century. Aristophanes, the fourth-century Athenian playwright, noted that lemon tree leaves were fashioned into wreaths to crown the heads of the gods. More than one thousand years earlier, when the Jews were cultivating a form of citrus in Palestine, they used the fruit as an integral part of the harvest celebration Succoth. When the Jews moved to various corners of the Roman empire, so did their lemon trees, and as a result lemons began to figure prominently, and continue to do so today, in the cuisines on all sides of the Mediterranean.

Choose large, bright yellow lemons with neither a hint of green (unripe or improperly stored) nor an orangey-gold color (old past their prime). The skin should be firm, unwrinkled, and blemish-free. It should also be thin. Thin-skinned citrus fruits are heavy for their size because they are juicier than their thick-skinned counterparts. Every part of the fruit is usable except the seeds and the pith, and each serves its own purpose. The zest, the shiny, bumpy yellow exterior which contains the rich lemon oil, adds intense flavor and aroma to recipes. Be careful when peeling it off to avoid the bitter white pith beneath. A sharp knife, a vegetable peeler, or a lemon zester can be used to remove the yellow and leave the white. To extract the maximum amount of juice from lemons and other citrus fruits, roll the fruit firmly under the palm of your hand on a counter or, if the skin is not needed in the recipe, pour boiling water over the uncut fruit and it will release more juice when squeezed. To retain vitamin C, add lemon juice to dishes after they are cooked.

My favorite way of preparing fish like red snapper is on a bed of lemons with pats of lemon herb butter, which add wonderful flavor. A variation particularly good for white fish, such as flounder, would be a bed of thinly sliced fennel. Top the fish with slices of lemon butter, garnish with the fennel fronds, and bake as indicated in the following recipe. Serve either fish with little red potatoes and asparagus for a memorable early spring meal. According to seafood sage Joe DiMauro of Mount Kisco Seafood, fish for baking or grilling is always used skin-side down.

Baked red snapper on a bed of lemons with lemon butter

Lemon butter

1 stick lightly salted butter, softened and whipped

1 tablespoon lemon juice

2 tablespoons minced parsley

2 tablespoons minced chives

1 scant teaspoon grated lemon zest

Baked fish

3 scrubbed lemons, cut into ¼-inch thick slices; discard ends

⅓ cup water

1½ pounds red snapper fillets

Salt and freshly ground (preferably white) pepper

Preheat oven to 350 degrees. Combine whipped butter, lemon juice, parsley, chives and zest thoroughly and shape in to a cylinder of 1½ inches in diameter. Cover with plastic wrap and refrigerate. Slice as needed. Line a shallow, ovenproof dish with a thin layer of lemon slices. Add water. Place red snapper fillets, skin-side down, to fit snugly in a single layer on top of lemon slices. Sprinkle with salt and pepper. Place 1 slice of the lemon herb butter (sliced about ½ inch thick) on each fillet. Cover dish with aluminum foil and bake for 12–15 minutes, depending on the thickness of the fish. Check after 10 minutes. Serve with more lemon butter slices on the side.

NOTE:
When buying lemons, look for large, bright yellow ones with neither a hint of green (unripe or improperly stored) or an orangey-gold color (past their prime).

Belgian endive
with ham and cheese sauce

4 large white Belgian endives; cut a thin slice from the

bottom

4 large ¼-inch thick ham slices (sandwich ham is fine)

4 tablespoons butter

4 tablespoons flour

1½ cup milk

1½ cup grated cheese (Gouda, Harvarti, or

Vermont cheddar)

In a saucepan large enough to hold the endives in one layer, add endives and just enough water to cover. Bring to a boil and cook for about 10 minutes until done (prick with a fork) but still very much together. Remove and cool until you are able to handle them. Preheat oven to 350 degrees. Meanwhile, butter a shallow ovenproof dish large enough to hold endives in one layer. Roll a slice of ham around each endive and place in the prepared dish. Make the cheese sauce as follows. In a saucepan, melt the butter, add flour, and stir with a whisk until combined. Slowly add milk and whisk to make a smooth sauce. Stir in the grated cheese and continue stirring until melted and combined. Pour over the ham rolls and bake for 15 minutes or until the sauce is bubbly and lightly browned. Serve with potatoes or bread.

Again, I am coming back to my childhood in the Netherlands and my mother's cooking. She would often serve this dish for Sunday dinner. I did not like it much as a child, but now I have come to appreciate the vegetable, especially when made with a good, creamy cheese sauce.

Peter's meatloaf

2 pounds lean ground beef

4 THICK slices whole grain bread without hard crust, soaked
in some milk and squeezed dry

2 eggs

1 medium onion, finely chopped, or less to taste

2 packages (10 ounces) frozen chopped spinach, thawed,
and squeezed dry OR 2 pounds baby spinach leaves,
briefly cooked and drained

4 tablespoons finely chopped parsley

Salt, pepper, and ground nutmeg

1 or 2 tomatoes, washed and sliced

Preheat oven to 350 degrees. In an electric mixer, combine ground beef, soaked bread, eggs, and onion and stir/beat to combine (this can be done by hand as well). Season with 1½ teaspoons salt and ¼ teaspoon pepper. In a separate bowl, combine spinach and parsley and season mixture lightly with salt and nutmeg. Use a 4 x 10-inch loaf pan. Place half the beef mixture in the bottom, top with the spinach mixture, and finish with a beef layer. Overlap slices of tomato on top. Bake for about 1 hour.

Serve with potatoes and (homemade) applesauce. (Simply cut 4 apples—any kind—into quarters, core, peel, and cook in a small saucepan with some water and a cinnamon stick. When the apples are done, about 10 minutes, remove stick and mash apples. Serve warm or cold.)

My friends love my meatloaf—it is my "signature dish," if you can use such a lofty term for such simple food. I do not use the traditional mixture of beef, veal, and pork, but just beef. The spinach layer adds moisture and one or two sliced tomatoes on top add color.

Pork chops with pears and blue cheese

Vegetable oil

4 thick pork chops

Salt and freshly ground pepper

2 large pears, quartered, cored and peeled

½ cup white wine or water

4 ounces crumbled blue cheese

In a frying pan, heat oil. Season pork chops with salt and pepper and fry until browned on both sides. In the meantime, cut each pear quarter lengthwise into 3 slices. Add pears to the browned chops, along with the wine or water. Cover pan, reduce heat, and cook for 15–20 minutes or until the chops are done. Uncover pan and sprinkle crumbled blue cheese on top. Turn off heat, replace the cover, and allow pan to stand for a few minutes. Potatoes and green beans are excellent accompaniments.

Pears are another locally grown winter fruit. Pears cut in half, core removed, and the hollows filled with a blue cheese and cream cheese mixture (see recipe in Summer section), together with a glass of Port, make a memorable winter dessert. There is nothing more fragrant and delicious than a perfectly ripe pear, but for this dish it is better to use pears that are not quite ripe so they will not fall apart in the cooking.

Stuffed Savoy cabbage rolls

1 Savoy cabbage

1 pound ground beef

2 slices whole grain bread, soaked in a
    little milk and squeezed dry

3 tablespoons finely chopped onions

2 tablespoons minced parsley

1 egg

3–4 ounces feta cheese, crumbled or cubed

Salt and freshly ground pepper to taste; keep in mind how
    salty the feta cheese is

Preheat oven to 350 degrees. Rinse cabbage and separate as many leaves as you will make rolls, about 8–10. Chop the rest of the cabbage to make a bed for the rolls. In a large pan, bring some water to a boil and drop in the cabbage leaves. Allow them to just wilt and remove with tongs. Repeat until all leaves are done. In a medium bowl, combine beef, bread, onion, parsley, and egg. Knead with your hand. Add cheese and lightly combine. Season as necessary. Place a cabbage leaf in front of you, put a small handful of beef mixture on top, and roll (no need for tying). You should be able to make 8–10 rolls with the filling. Butter a shallow baking dish, add chopped cabbage in one layer, and place the rolls on top. Pour in ¼ cup water and cover the dish with aluminum foil. Bake for about 40–50 minutes or until done (cut into one roll to check). Serve with potatoes; I also like another vegetable with the meal, such as carrots sprinkled with lots of parsley.

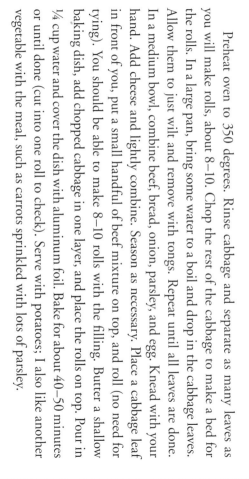

I have always used round, green cabbages for cabbage rolls and it is quite a chore to neatly separate the leaves. I tried making the rolls with Savoy cabbage (the crinkled-leaf variety) and found it to be much easier.

17

Vegetables, fruits, or grains

These days, there is very little difference in the availability of summer or winter vegetables and the seasons seem to blur. We need to make our own efforts to support Hudson Valley farms and eat winter vegetables whenever possible. I made some less obvious choices by giving you recipes for curly endive, leeks, and beautiful beets, which now come in two colors. While using oranges seems to negate the purpose of eating locally, citrus fruits are a quintessential winter staple with a long history in the Hudson Valley. There is even an eighteenth-century letter in the New York State Library in which a mother in Albany thanks her son in New York City for sending her six oranges. I could not resist giving you a recipe for stewing them. The last recipe for sweet potatoes and apples flavored with sage makes a true winter dish.

Curly endive with mashed potatoes and bacon

Mashed potatoes, enough for 4; keep warm
4–6 slices crisp cooked bacon, crumbled
1 medium head curly endive, thoroughly washed
Salt, pepper, and a dash of white vinegar

Cover mashed potatoes and keep warm. Cut the head of endive in thin strips and add to the potatoes, together with bacon. Warm gently; the endive should wilt slightly, but still be raw. Season with salt, pepper, and a small dash of vinegar for a clean, fresh taste.

NOTE:
This is a simple dish that is particularly good with juicy, grilled burgers.

Curly endive, which some call chicory, is a sturdy leaf vegetable that can be chopped, washed, and cooked with the water that clings to the leaves, just like spinach. You can add a few tablespoons of butter and thicken the little sauce slightly with cornstarch and season with salt, pepper, and nutmeg. Another way to use it is in this mashed potato mixture.

Leeks

2 pounds leek, with some inner green leaves (see below)

2 tablespoons butter

Cornstarch

Salt, pepper, and white vinegar

Cut leeks in ½-inch slices and wash. They are often quite dirty, so rub them between your hands while washing to remove the grit. Place in a saucepan and add 1 cup water. Cover and cook for about 15 minutes. Check frequently to make sure they do not cook dry. When soft, add butter and thicken the cooking water with 2 teaspoons cornstarch mixed with 2 tablespoons of water. Season the dish with salt, pepper, and vinegar, to taste.

NOTE:
This is excellent with pork or brisket of beef.

Hudson Valley farm markets have an abundance of beautiful fat, long leeks, yet they are seldom used as the star of the table. As in the previous recipe, vinegar is added to accent the flavor.

Red and golden beets

4 EACH red and golden beets
(about 3 pounds)

2 tablespoons butter, divided

1 teaspoon sugar, divided

½ teaspoon ground cloves, divided

4 tablespoons minced parsley, divided

Salt and pepper

Cook the two kinds of beets separately in water to cover. When they can be pierced through with a fork, drain and cool. Rub off the thin outer skin and slice ½ inch thick. Clean the pans and return the beets, again separately, to their own pans. On low heat, add 1 tablespoon butter, ½ teaspoon sugar, and ¼ teaspoon cloves to each pan and stir to combine. Taste the beets (the cloves should not overshadow the beet flavor, so be careful if you want to add more) and season with salt and pepper. Add 2 tablespoons of parsley to each pan, cover, and cook for 2 or 3 minutes. To serve, you can either combine them in one serving dish or you can spoon the red beets on one side of a shallow dish and the golden ones on the other. Yes, they are worth the work.

Lately we see more and more golden beets. The mixture of the traditional red vegetable with this newer one is a visual delight, so I cook them in separate pans and carefully combine them when ready to serve.

Stewed oranges

3 navel oranges, peeled and broken in half

Zest and juice of 1 orange

Generous pinch EACH ground cloves and nutmeg

Juice of 2 more navel oranges

Place the 6 orange halves in a pan large enough to hold them in one layer. Sprinkle with zest and spices. Pour on the juice and place the pan on low heat. Cover and gently cook for 30 minutes. Remove from heat and cool. This makes a nice side dish for poultry, ham, or pork chops.

I found a mention of stewed oranges as a side dish in a nineteenth-century Dutch cookbook. I liked the idea and put together this recipe.

Sweet potatoes with apples and sage

4 medium sweet potatoes, peeled and cut into
   1-inch chunks (about 4 cups)

2 apples (Mutsu or Crispin, actually the same apple and
   grown in the Hudson Valley, or use Golden Delicious)

3 tablespoons vegetable oil

½ teaspoon sugar

1 teaspoon salt

½–1 teaspoon ground sage

Preheat oven to 375 degrees. Cut apples in quarters, core, and peel and cut each quarter crosswise into three parts. Combine with sweet potatoes on a baking sheet with a rim. In a small bowl, mix oil, sugar, salt, and sage and brush mixture generously onto the potatoes and apples. Bake for 15 minutes, stir and brush with more of the oil mixture. Return to the oven and check at 10-minute intervals. Total cooking time will be about 30–35 minutes or until the potatoes are soft. When ready to serve, dust the potatoes lightly with more sage and serve.

NOTE:
These potatoes are particularly delicious when paired with the stewed oranges from the preceding recipe.

You probably have sage on your spice rack to use in stuffing; you can also use it for sweet potatoes since their tastes complement each other beautifully. Roast the potatoes in the oven to slightly caramelize them and bring out their sweetness.

18

Desserts

With the following five recipes I lean heavily on the valley's Dutch roots and include a cornstarch pudding, an almond-paste-filled puff pastry, and a specialty from the town where I was born, Utrecht, in the center of the Netherlands. Milk-based porridges, puddings, and *vla*, a runny pudding, were and are favorite Dutch dishes. The early settlers brought horses, pigs, sheep, and especially cows with them and used their milk for porridges and for making butter and cheese. The butter was used not only to top bread or for frying, but, when melted, as part of a rather sour dressing for coleslaw.

We cannot talk about fall and winter desserts without including at least one apple recipe. To us a trip to nearby Salinger's Orchards in Brewster means shopping for apples and a favorite outing. When you enter the barn, it has the most wonderful smell of fruit, cider, fresh doughnuts, and other baked goods. The current owner, Bruce Salinger, told me that his grandfather bought the acreage in 1901, raised breeding chickens there for other farms and started the orchard. His wife Maureen is responsible for all the baked goods that are sold at the orchard and people come from near and far for her pies.

If you are up north, do not miss out on a trip to Indian Ladder Farms in Altamont. Aside from apples, it has other farm products such as berries and vegetables, but also a fun gift shop and café. Peter Ten Eyck explained how his farm was the first in Albany County to be chosen for a New York State program in which the state buys the development rights to select properties. Indian Ladder Farms' acreage will forever remain only for agricultural use, which ensures that part of the state's "soil bank" will be preserved for later generations.

Apple-nut surprise

Enough cooking apple halves (such as Mutsu a.k.a. Crispin) to cover the bottom of a 10-inch deep dish pie plate or use a 9-inch square dish (probably 7 halves)

4 tablespoons butter (plus more for buttering the dish)

½–1 cup sugar, depending on sweetness of the apples

3 eggs, separated

4 slices white bread

Milk

1 teaspoon EACH lemon juice and ground cinnamon

1 cup coarsely chopped pecans or walnuts

Heavy cream whipped with some sugar (sugar optional)

Preheat oven to 350 degrees. Butter the pie plate or square dish. Peel apples and cut in half crosswise. Core; they will now look like big donuts. Arrange the halved apples in the dish with the cut side up. With an electric mixer, beat the butter and sugar until fluffy and add the egg yolks one at a time, beating well after each addition. Soak the slices of bread, crust and all, in just enough milk to soften bread. Squeeze dry and add to the butter mixture along with the lemon juice, cinnamon, and nuts. Beat the egg whites until stiff and add them to this mixture, stirring them in with an under/over motion. Spread the topping evenly over the apples. (Sprinkle lightly with some sugar, if you wish.) Bake at 350 degrees for 30–40 minutes or until browned and puffy. Top each serving with whipped cream, if desired. The recipe serves 6.

To say that apple-nut surprise is a pudding would not define it properly. It is not a pie, a cake, a cobbler, or a grunt. To make the "surprise," apples are cut in half and form the base for a chewy topping of nuts, bread, and eggs. Serve it hot or cold. It is unusual and unusually good, especially with a large dollop of whipped cream.

Cherry *kuchen*

1¼ cup flour

1 teaspoon baking powder

½ cup sugar

1 tablespoon butter, softened

1 egg

½ cup milk

1 can (14.5 ounces) sour pitted cherries, drained

Frosting

1 cup confectioners' sugar

4 tablespoons butter, softened

1 teaspoon vanilla

Preheat oven to 375 degrees. In the bowl of an electric mixer, combine flour, baking powder, sugar, butter, egg, and milk and beat at low speed until the dough is formed. Transfer to a buttered 9-inch square dish. Put cherries on top in a single layer. Bake for 25 minutes or until golden. In the meantime, make the frosting. In a small bowl, combine confectioners' sugar, butter, and vanilla and stir to make a smooth frosting. Remove the cake from the oven; it is done when a toothpick inserted comes out clean. Spread the frosting while the cake is still hot. Cut into squares for serving.

To celebrate the large German population of the valley—Palatine Germans came here in the early eighteenth century—I am including this recipe for a kuchen with a topping of sour cherries and butter frosting. It was given to me by a reader, the late Dottie Fox, at the time from Mamaroneck. Many in that area will remember Dottie's excellent baked goods, for which she often used one of her mother's recipes like this one.

Puff pastry sticks
filled with almond paste

1 sheet commercial puff pastry (I favor Pepperidge Farm brand), thawed according to package instructions

4 ounces canned almond paste (cut into small pieces) too finely processed)

1 large egg, beaten with 1 tablespoon water

Preheat the oven to 400 degrees. Carefully cut pastry sheet in half (which yields 2 pieces of about 4½ x 9 inches). Set aside 2 tablespoons of the egg mixture in a small dish. In an electric mixer, combine almond paste (cut into small pieces) and the rest of the egg and beat to combine. Divide in half and roll one half into a sausage of 8 inches long and place on one of the puff pastry halves. Repeat with remaining almond paste. Brush the sides of the pastry with the egg mixture and roll over to encase the almond paste. Make sure the seam is secure and fold the ends as if it were a package and tuck under. Brush both sticks with the egg wash. Transfer to a buttered baking sheet (seam-side down) and bake for about 30 minutes. Check after 20 minutes and turn the baking sheet in the oven. The sticks are done when golden brown and puffed. Cool on a rack.

Puff pastry is wrapped around a roll of almond paste in this recipe. It makes either a stick or, when a longer piece is used, can be formed into a letter as you can see in the photograph on the back cover. In the Midwest, where the nineteenth-century wave of Dutch immigration took place, particularly in Pella, Iowa, and Holland, Michigan, "letters" are still sold around holiday time as they are in the Netherlands.

Rum raisin pudding

2 cups milk

½ teaspoon vanilla extract

2 tablespoons butter

½ cup golden raisins

1 egg

3 tablespoons dark rum

4 tablespoons cornstarch

4 tablespoons sugar

Rinse a saucepan with water and pour in the milk and vanilla extract. Add butter and raisins and slowly bring to a boil over low heat. In the meantime, in a small bowl, whisk the egg with the rum until well combined. Spoon cornstarch and sugar in another small bowl and whisk in the egg/rum mixture. Pour in a little of the heated milk and combine. When milk boils, pour the cornstarch mixture into the milk and whisk continuously over low heat for 2–3 minutes to remove the raw starch taste. Rinse a serving bowl with water and pour in the pudding. Cover with plastic wrap and cool. Refrigerate and serve cold with lots of whipped cream.

Pudding and vla, runny pudding sold in bottles like milk, are the quintessential Dutch desserts at home. Millions of liters are consumed each year. After all, the Netherlands is a dairy country and milk products are favorite foods. This recipe might convince you that those Dutch know what they are doing.

Utrecht darling (heart-shaped pastry)

4 cups flour

1 teaspoon baking powder

1 teaspoon salt

1 teaspoon cardamom

½ teaspoon EACH ground ginger, nutmeg, and cloves

2 cups light brown sugar

2 cups milk

½ cup (scant) raisins

¼ cup candied citron, minced

¾ cup candied orange peel, minced

2 tablespoons candied red cherries, chopped

Extra citron, orange peel, angelica, and cherries for

    decoration

Glaze

1 cup confectioners' sugar mixed with 4 teaspoons Kirsch

    for each heart

Preheat oven to 350 degrees. Butter a 9-inch heart form. In an electric mixer, combine flour, baking powder, salt, spices, and sugar. Mix for a minute to combine. Add milk, followed by the fruit, and beat to combine. Fill the heart form with HALF

Here is an old recipe that was part of the timeworn custom that on local fair day (kermis) a young man would give his beloved a heart-shaped koek or cake. The hearts are easy to make and are a lot of fun to decorate with the most colorful candied fruit you can find; they should be a bit gaudy—"bright is beautiful" in this case. Nowadays they make a perfect gift for your favorite Valentine. This recipe makes two hearts.

of the batter; refrigerate the remaining batter. Bake for 40 minutes (check after 30) or until a toothpick inserted comes out clean. Cool on a rack for 5 minutes; remove from form. Butter the form again and spoon in remaining batter and bake. When cakes are cool, work with one cake at a time and mix confectioners' sugar with Kirsch, adding a little more if necessary to make a smooth, thick glaze. Spread on the top of one cake only. Decorate immediately by creating small flowers with the candied fruit. Make the decorations as colorful as possible by using citron, red and green candied cherries, angelica, and dark or golden raisins. Make a new batch of glaze for the second cake and repeat.

19

Cookies, small treats
to enjoy by the fire

I n winter, we settle by the fire after dinner and there is nothing nicer than having a plate of home-baked cookies at hand. Bourbon balls, macaroons, and rum molasses or spiced cookies all go well with an after-dinner cup of coffee or tea.

The historic house museum of Van Cortlandt Manor in Croton-on-Hudson still gives hearth cooking classes that are a joy to attend. I have taken many of them over the years, but the first one I took some twenty years ago was all about confectionery. I learned to make the following delicious macaroons. The recipe is adapted from Joanne Van Cortlandt's files. Mrs. Van Cortlandt did not have access to commercial almond paste and made her own by pounding almonds, rosewater, and sugar in a mortar with a pestle. The paste is a convenient, modern-day shortcut and so is the use of a blender or food processor.

Almond macaroons

1 7-ounce roll of almond paste/marzipan

2 egg whites, lightly beaten with a fork

½ cup all-purpose flour

Preheat oven to 325 degrees. Cut almond paste into small pieces and put into blender or food processor. Add flour and then egg whites. Process until you have a thick, smooth paste. Butter and flour a baking sheet. Use 2 teaspoons of dough for each cookie and drop on prepared sheet and shape with the spoon into small round cookies. (It is a sticky job!) Bake for 15–20 minutes, until cookies are a very light brown on top and golden on the edges. This recipe makes about 2 dozen cookies. These are best on the day they are made, but can be refreshed by putting them in a 300 degree oven for 10 minutes. Cool and serve.

Bourbon balls

1½ cups vanilla wafers, crushed

1 cup confectioners' sugar

1 cup pecans, coarsely chopped

2 tablespoons cocoa

2 tablespoons light corn syrup

¼ cup bourbon

Granulated sugar for coating, or use cocoa powder

Thoroughly combine all six ingredients in a large bowl. Form into 1-inch balls and roll in granulated sugar. Chill and serve. Balls store well in the refrigerator. This recipe makes 30 bourbon balls.

Bourbon balls are a southern treat. I learned to make them when we lived in Raleigh, North Carolina, before we moved to the Hudson Valley and they have been part of our holiday cookie tray ever since. I also make the balls during the year when I have visitors from Europe—they are always received with glee as being "so American." Because no cooking is involved, it is a fun (but, I grant you, a bit messy) project to do by the fire.

Rum and molasses crinkles

¾ cup butter, softened

1 cup dark brown sugar

1 egg

¼ cup molasses

¼ cup dark rum

2½ cups flour

2 teaspoons baking soda

¼ teaspoon salt

½ teaspoon cloves

1 teaspoon EACH ground cinnamon and ginger

Beat together butter and sugar. Add the egg, molasses, and rum and combine thoroughly. In a separate bowl, sift together dry ingredients and stir into butter/sugar mixture. Chill the dough overnight. Preheat oven to 350 degrees. Roll into 1-inch balls. Pour some sugar in a small bowl and dip top of each dough ball in sugar and place about 3 inches apart on a greased baking sheet. Sprinkle each cookie with 2 drops of water. Bake just until set, about 15 minutes. This recipe makes 3 dozen cookies.

Rum and molasses are by-products of sugar cane. Rum is fermented cane juice and molasses is the dark residue of sugar fabrication. Seventeenth- and eighteenth-century Hudson Valley traders were heavily involved in the sugar trade with the Caribbean. The rum in the recipe above creates an underlayer of flavor for the molasses. These cookies are not for the faint-hearted, but they are very good.

Spiced cookies (Dutch *speculaas*)

1½ cups all-purpose flour

½ teaspoon baking soda

1 cup brown sugar (do not pack)

1½ tablespoon *speculaas* spices (see next page; keep leftover

    spice mixture in a tightly closed jar)

Pinch of salt

3–4 tablespoons shaved almonds

1 egg

1½ tablespoons milk

1¼ sticks (10 tablespoons) butter, softened

These spiced cookies are sometimes called "windmill cookies" because they are molded in wooden cake molds in a windmill shape. In this recipe, we simply cut them into squares. The recipe was given to me by my Dutch friend Harry Veenendaal. It came from her grandfather who was a baker in Dieren in the province of Gelderland (for which Guilderland, New York, is named). The flavor is best when the dough is allowed to rest overnight. After the cookies are baked, they improve with age as well. Store them in an airtight container.

Speculaas spices

4 teaspoons ground cinnamon

1 teaspoon freshly grated nutmeg

1 teaspoon ground cloves

½ teaspoon ground anise seed

½ teaspoon freshly ground pepper

¼ teaspoon ground cardamom

In a small bowl, mix spices and set aside. In a large bowl, mix flour, baking soda, sugar, almonds, and spices. In a cup or bowl, beat together egg and milk and pour into flour mixture; add butter and knead by hand until a fairly stiff dough is formed. You can also combine the ingredients in a food processor and process until dough is formed. Wrap in plastic wrap and refrigerate overnight. The next day, on a buttered baking sheet, pat out the dough a little less than ½ inch thick and use a rolling pin to smooth the top. Place in a cold oven, set at 325 degrees, and bake 35–40 minutes. Remove and cut into squares. Transfer to racks and cool.

Zebras (striped chocolate and vanilla cookies)

1 cup butter, softened

¾ cup confectioners' sugar

⅛ teaspoon salt

2 cups all-purpose flour

1 tablespoon unsweetened cocoa powder

½ teaspoon vanilla extract

In the bowl of an electric mixer, cream butter with the confectioners' sugar and the salt, add flour, and beat until the mixture holds together. Divide in half and transfer half the dough to a small bowl. Stir in the cocoa powder. Add the vanilla extract to the other half and combine. Wrap doughs separately in plastic wrap and chill for 30 minutes. On a lightly floured surface, roll out each dough into a 6-inch square, cut each square into three 2-inch wide strips, and brush strips lightly with water. Stack the strips, alternating light and dark layers on top of each other. Roll the stacked dough into a 9 × 2½-inch rectangle and wrap and chill for another 30 minutes. Preheat oven to 350 degrees. Place the dough on a cutting board and cut across into ¼-inch thick slices. Arrange on a buttered baking sheet and bake for about 15 minutes or until the cookies are light gold. Transfer to racks and proceed with the other cookies. This recipe makes 30 cookies.

What else could you call cookies that have light and dark stripes but zebras? The same name is traditionally applied to a snack of dark buttered bread layered with creamy Gouda cheese (see chapter 5 of the Summer section). This is a most delicious, crisp, buttery cookie.

20

The little extras that make any occasion special

Adding a homemade relish or chutney to an otherwise ordinary meal suddenly makes it more festive and enjoyable. The flavors in the following recipes will accent a variety of foods. The strawberry-pineapple preserves are particularly good on hot baking powder biscuits.

The first recipe requires no cooking. None of the usual long simmering is necessary to obtain a tasty mixture that will give a sunny, fresh flavor to winter foods. I prefer it slightly heated, and warm a small dish of it in the microwave before serving.

Caribbean chutney

1 8-ounce can crushed pineapple

2 oranges, peeled, sectioned, and chopped

2 tablespoons dark raisins

2 tablespoons whole almonds or walnuts

½ teaspoon grated fresh ginger

¼ teaspoon curry powder or more to taste

Combine the ingredients. Allow the chutney to stand at room temperature for at least an hour. Serve at room temperature or slightly warmed.

Fresh mango and strawberry relish

1 pint strawberries, thoroughly washed and diced

1 ripe mango, peeled and diced

2 small cloves garlic, minced

2 tablespoons fresh basil, chopped

½ teaspoon ground cumin

¼ cup champagne or white wine vinegar

4 tablespoons Hudson Valley honey

Salt and freshly ground pepper to taste

In a medium bowl, combine first five ingredients. Stir together vinegar, honey, salt, and pepper and pour on the mixture. Combine thoroughly and serve cold or slightly warmed.

The recipe above was given to me years ago by my Dutch friend and accomplished chef/master baker Peter de Jong. He likes to pair the relish with crispy fried fish such as flounder. It is so quickly made that you can use it to perk up any meal. I especially like it with poultry. The hard strawberries we find in the supermarkets in the winter are particularly suited for this use (you can also slice them and add to a salad), and supermarkets sell basil even in winter.

Orange vinaigrette

⅔ cup white wine vinegar

⅓ cup olive or vegetable oil

Juice of 2 blood oranges

1 teaspoon EACH sugar and salt or more to taste

½ teaspoon freshly ground pepper

Combine all ingredients in a jar and shake vigorously. *Note*: It is better not to add salad herbs to this dressing since they lose much of their flavor. Instead, sprinkle them directly onto the salad, toss with the dressing, and serve.

One of the joys of winter for us in the East is when blood oranges come into season. Often local organizations sell boxes as a fundraiser. Blood orange juice is a delicious addition to sauces or to use in the following vinaigrette. If blood oranges are not available, use navel oranges, lemons, or limes—each gives the mixture a different flavor.

Spiced cranberries

1 medium Granny Smith apple, or other green apple,
scrubbed

1 pound fresh cranberries

¾ cup white wine vinegar or white distilled vinegar

⅓ cup water

¼ cup dark brown sugar, packed

1½ teaspoons ground cinnamon

½ teaspoon ground cloves

Grated zest of 1 orange

Cut apple into quarters and core. Dice apple as neatly as possible. Combine all ingredients in a medium saucepan and bring to a boil. Turn down the heat and simmer for about 20 minutes, stirring frequently, until cranberries are well done and mixture is thick. Cool and taste; add sugar as needed. Serve cold or at room temperature. Refrigerate leftovers; this mixture keeps well.

Freeze a couple of extra bags of cranberries. You might like to make this side dish even after the holidays. It goes well with poultry, but also with pork or ham.

Strawberry-pineapple preserves

1 quart strawberries, hulled and thickly sliced

4 cups chopped fresh pineapple (about half a pineapple;
serve the rest sliced with dollops of sweetened whipped
cream)

2 pounds of sugar

Combine fruits and let stand for half an hour. In a low, open pan, mix fruits and sugar and bring to a boil. Cook briskly, stirring frequently, for 20 or 30 minutes or until a dollop dropped on a plate jells when cooled. Cool and put into clean jars that have been rinsed with boiling water, refrigerate, or store in freezer containers and freeze.

This recipe is foolproof—no matter how it turns out, it can still be used. If it is thick as a jam should be, spread it on hot toast or baking powder biscuits; if it is runny, pour it on those biscuits or use it as a topping for pancakes or ice cream. It is always just delicious. Hawaiian pineapples are in season in April and May just when we see strawberries in the stores in the East. April and May just when we see strawberries in the stores in the East. April still has enough cold days when you'd like to stand in the kitchen to make something for the months to come.